FOSTERING A... ...KING
A Guide for ... ...ades 6–10

Mark Driscoll

Heinemann
Portsmouth, NH

Heinemann

361 Hanover Street
Portsmouth, NH 03801–3912
http://www.heinemann.com

Offices and agents throughout the world

Library of Congress Cataloging-in-Publication Data
Driscoll, Mark J.
    Fostering algebraic thinking : a guide for teachers, grades 6–10 / Mark Driscoll.
      p.   cm.
    Includes bibliographical references and index.
    ISBN 0-325-00154-5
    1. Algebra—Study and teaching (Secondary)   I. Title.
  QA159.D74   1999
  512'.071'2—dc21   98-51138
                                                   CIP

Editors: Hilary Breed Van Dusen and Leigh Peake
Production: Elizabeth Valway
Cover design: Jenny Jensen Greenleaf
Manufacturing: Louise Richardson

Printed in the United States of America on acid-free paper
11 10 09   EB   17 18

CONTENTS

ACKNOWLEDGMENTS

Many people helped in the production of this book. Primary among those was Sydney Foster, research assistant in the Linked Learning in Mathematics project. Not only did Sydney search far and wide for the mathematics activities that appear throughout the book and write the solutions sections for many, she also helped to keep the writing on schedule, coordinated draft reviews, incorporated review data into the text, did thorough editing of early drafts, and contributed significantly to the design of the book's chapter structure. Sydney was much more colleague to me than assistant in putting the book together, and I am very grateful for her support and help.

Also helpful in providing feedback and suggestions for early drafts were Linked Learning teachers from Milwaukee Public Schools: Joan Grampp, Margie Klingsporn, Jayne Patterson, and Eric Schluter. In addition, Linked Learning colleagues Jack Moyer, Judi Zawojewski, and Lynn Goldsmith gave valuable feedback that helped to set and keep us on course. Tony Artuso at the Education Development Center (EDC) was very helpful in the practical aspects of preparing the manuscript for publication.

EDC colleagues Al Cuoco, Paul Goldenberg, and June Mark were influential, and I want to acknowledge their help. Their efforts in the past few years to describe mathematical habits of mind and to emphasize their importance in school mathematics inspired much of the work represented in the book.

Lastly, for the ideas in this book, much is owed to the hundreds of teachers who have participated in our projects, along with their students, from Dayton, Durham, Los Angeles, Memphis, Milwaukee, Pittsburgh, St. Louis, San Diego, San Francisco, and Worcester. The book is enriched by their stories and student work, and by the questions and concerns they have communicated, which form the framework of the book. We are very grateful.

INTRODUCTION

This book is written for teachers who want to reflect on, and perhaps redirect, their thinking about the learning and teaching of prealgebra and algebra, in light of the movement to base curriculum, instruction, and assessment on clearly defined standards. By focusing on explicit criteria for what is important to learn, the K through 12 standards movement has shifted the attention of educators from teaching toward learning. In this book we try to follow that shift by emphasizing learning issues around mathematical thinking as much as strategies for teaching mathematical thinking.

The book's ideas are derived in good measure from three teacher-enhancement projects in which we at the Education Development Center (EDC) have been involved[1]: the Linked Learning in Mathematics project, the Leadership for Urban Mathematics Reform (LUMR) project, and the Assessment Communities of Teachers (ACT) project. A central belief underlying our work has been that attention to learning, balanced with attention to teaching, is necessary in mathematics teachers' professional development. This is different from the norm. Typically, even when staff development focuses on standards-based mathematics education, the thrust of teachers' work together has been to translate what they hear and experience into instructional terms. In part, this phenomenon is due to the dominance that "how-to" considerations have had in teachers' professional development over considerations about how learning happens.

In our work with teachers, our goal has been to provide something different: experiences that prompt deep and personal reflections about learning, and that cause teachers to bring to the surface the mindsets that underlie their theories about learning that guide their own learning and, eventually, color the way they teach. As a result, the approaches to professional development emphasize productive habits of thinking, such as those that are associated with the effective understanding and use of algebra. In addition, we have emphasized the analysis of student work, using habits of thinking as criteria for analysis. Discussions are structured to invite teachers to reflect on their own thinking, as well as that of colleagues and the students whose work they analyze. They are structured to measure the gaps between what characterizes productive algebraic thinking and the thinking patterns that typically characterize students' development of algebraic thinking, as reflected in student work.

We believe that grounding professional development in the understanding of productive habits of thinking

- gives substance to efforts at cross-grades articulation. In fact, the Linked Learning in Mathematics and LUMR projects have worked with mixed groups of middle-grades and high school teachers, often analyzing cross-grade student work on the same mathematics task.

- creates opportunities for action toward equity in schools, in the sense that student efficacy can be grounded in teachers' knowledge of how to foster the development of productive habits of algebraic thinking. With its emphasis on student thinking and learning in the analysis of student work, as opposed to emphasizing only whether the students "got it," fresh insights are often gained about what student work reveals about thinking patterns. In turn, the focus on threads of productive mathematical thinking as they develop across grades makes it possible for teachers and students to become agents in this development.

So much of the work on understanding habits of thinking would have limited appeal and value to teachers if it didn't lead eventually to decisions about classroom practice. It is one thing to see threads of algebraic thinking in a student response or to notice gaps in thinking; it is quite another thing to know how to teach the student to develop his or her thinking in productive ways. Much of our project work with teachers has included discussions, often based on analysis of student work, about the gap between effective mathematical thinking and what students reveal about their thinking. We have noticed a set of critical issues that seem to arise naturally in these discussions. These issues, emerging typically from the inferences teachers make about the way a particular student approached a problem, become the bridges to talking about classroom practice, and form the organizational framework of this book.

The first chapter sets the stage for the remaining chapters by describing our perspective on algebraic thinking and by providing a framework for the use of classroom questions to foster the development of algebraic thinking in students from grades 6 through 10. Each subsequent chapter uses the following elements to address its particular focus issue:

- An account, from the learner's perspective, of why the issue is important and how it connects to our algebraic-thinking framework. Whenever possible and appropriate, the accounts are supported by references to learning research. Also, on occasion, we have been able to support the descriptions with samples of student work gathered in our projects.

- An account, from the teacher's perspective, of some key classroom considerations in order to support students' growth of algebraic thinking. Particular attention is given to the kinds of questions teachers can ask students.

Chapter 1	Besides serving the purpose of orienting the reader to our approach to algebraic thinking through three algebraic habits of mind, this chapter addresses the role of teacher questioning in the fostering of algebraic thinking. In particular, the questions: *What kinds of open questions can foster algebraic thinking, and when is it best to use them?*
Chapter 2	One traditional definition of *algebra* is "generalized arithmetic." This points to the need for careful bridging between arithmetic and algebra. *What can be done to help students build on arithmetic computational skills to develop their algebraic thinking?*
Chapter 3	Similarly, there are mathematical experiences that students have in early grades that are not particularly arithmetical or computational, like those related to number sense. *What can be done to help students build on number sense to develop their algebraic thinking?*
Chapter 4	Any effective bridging from elementary school mathematics to algebra will involve generalization about the operations being used in arithmetic. *What can be done to foster operation sense or the capacity to generalize about number-system structure?*
Chapter 5	Similarly, as students engage with functions and relations in prealgebra and algebra, they need to know how to generalize in that domain. *What can be done to foster the capacity to generalize about functional relations?*
Chapter 6	Symbolic representation and manipulation are the lifeblood of algebra. *How and when should students be expected to engage in symbolic representation and manipulation in algebra?*
Chapter 7	Really productive algebraic thinkers can let their thinking flow easily among different algebraic representations. *How can students be helped to understand, use, and link multiple representations?*

• A few brief stories from our projects. We have found that a critical element in teachers informing their teaching with a greater understanding of learning has been their willingness to explore their own thinking. Therefore, whenever possible, we have incorporated brief stories from the projects about teachers' explorations into learning. These stories are not intended to describe the projects from which they originate, as much as they are intended to convey some of what was learned about algebraic thinking, through the teachers' mathematical explorations and discussions.

• A set of mathematics activities that might prompt similar reflections by readers about their own algebraic thinking, for possible use with their students. Each activity is accompanied by a discussion of its solution, pointers to possible extensions, and connections to the algebraic-thinking framework. Many of the activities are suitable for students across the 6 through 10 grade span.

• A brief list of references for further reading

Note

1. All three are or were National Science Foundation teacher-enhancement projects: 1. Linked Learning in Mathematics: Marquette University (1997–),

ESI-9619366, involves Milwaukee teachers; 2. Leadership for Urban Mathematics Reform (LUMR): Education Development Center (1994–1997), ESI-9353449, involved teachers in Durham, Los Angeles, Milwaukee, St. Louis, San Diego, and Worcester; 3. Assessment Communities of Teachers (ACT): Pittsburgh Public Schools (1994–1997), ESI-9353622, involved teachers in Dayton, Memphis, Milwaukee, Pittsburgh, San Diego, and San Francisco.

1 Developing Algebraic Habits of Mind
A Framework for Classroom Questions Aimed at Understanding Student Thinking

Because algebra comprises so many mathematical features, the term *algebraic thinking* defies simple definition. Generally, those who use the term do so after first choosing to concentrate on particular features, and then concern themselves with the thinking that those features demand. For example, some focus on the abstract features that distinguish algebra from arithmetic. With that perspective, they might characterize algebraic thinking as "the ability to operate on an unknown quantity as if the quantity was known, in contrast to arithmetic reasoning which involves operations on known quantities" (Langrall & Swafford 1997, 2). Others focus on the important role that functions play in algebra, and may characterize algebraic thinking as the capacity to represent quantitative situations so that relations among variables become apparent. Yet others may have problem solving as their point of reference for thinking about algebra and for thinking algebraically, and might concern themselves with how problem solvers model problems.

Our perspective has been influenced by our work with groups of teachers representing grades 6 through 10, so we emphasize habits of thinking that can begin developing in the prealgebra years and, if nurtured, can serve the learning of formal algebra as well. When people think algebraically in order to solve problems, explore, and so on, certain habits of thinking come into play. This chapter discusses three habits that seem to be critical to developing power in algebraic thinking. The list isn't meant to be comprehensive. However, we have no doubt that by learning to attend, in an ongoing fashion, to these several habits—in our own and in students' mathematical work—we will be better prepared to help students succeed in algebra.

A facility with algebraic thinking includes being able to think about *functions* and how they work, and to think about the impact that a system's *structure* has on calculations. These two aspects of algebraic thinking are facilitated by certain habits of mind (Figure 1–1):

- **Doing–Undoing.** Effective algebraic thinking sometimes involves reversibility (i.e., being able to undo mathematical processes as well as do them). In effect, it is the capacity not only to use a process to get to a goal, but

FIGURE 1–1. *Three Alegbraic Thinking Habits of Mind*

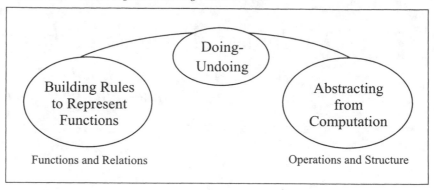

also to understand the process well enough to work backward from the answer to the starting point. So, for example, in a traditional algebraic setting, algebraic thinkers cannot only solve an equation such as $9x^2 - 16 = 0$, but also answer the question, "What is an equation with solutions 4/3 and −4/3?"

- **Building Rules to Represent Functions.** Critical to algebraic thinking is the capacity to recognize patterns and organize data to represent situations in which input is related to output by well-defined functional rules. For example, here is a functional rule that is computation-based: "Take an input number, multiply it by 4 and subtract 3." This habit of mind is a natural complement to Doing–Undoing, in that the capacity to understand how a functional rule works in reverse generally makes it a more accessible and useful process.

- **Abstracting from Computation.** This is the capacity to think about computations independently of particular numbers that are used. One of the most evident characteristics of algebra has always been its abstractness. But, just what is being abstracted? To answer this, a good case can be made that thinking algebraically involves being able to *think about computations freed from the particular numbers they are tied to in arithmetic*—that is, abstracting system regularities from computation. For example, students invoke this habit of mind when they realize that they can regroup numbers into pairs that equal 101 to make the following computation simpler: "Compute: $1 + 2 + 3 + \ldots + 100$." There is a suggestion of Doing–Undoing here, as well, in the recognition that 101 can be decomposed into $100 + 1$; $99 + 2$; $98 + 3$; and so on.

Guiding Questions

Habits of mind develop as the thinker pays attention, over and over again, to "what works" (e.g., what helps in solving problems or what can explain the regularity in a particular pattern) and looks for cues in new situations that previously used approaches may help. Often, the cueing may occur through "guiding questions" that the thinker asks himself. For example, consider these three basic algebraic-thinking questions: How does this process work in reverse? How are things changing in this situation? What are my operation shortcut options to get from here to there? The first and second questions may spur the representation of functions, when that is appropriate; the third may help to spur abstract thinking about calculation, when that is appropriate.

Table 1–1 is a beginning list of guiding questions for each of the three habits of mind. Throughout this book, we try to illustrate the usefulness of the questions with various mathematics activities and examples of student work. The questions in Table 1–1 have developed in our projects over time, and they keep developing and changing as teachers engage with the notion of algebraic-thinking habits of mind and experiment with questions that can help to foster their development in students.

The Role of Classroom Questions

If, as is our belief, these habits of algebraic thinking can be learned, what should teachers be doing to foster the learning? Based on our best information, we can say that productive instruction probably combines the following:

- Consistent modeling of algebraic thinking. For example, in summarizing student responses to a mathematical activity, a teacher might try to make explicit what students have left implicit in their thinking: "So, you decided to try your rule on some larger numbers to see if it would work."

- Giving well-timed pointers to students that help them shift or expand their thinking, or that help them pay attention to what is important. For example, the students of a Linked Learning middle-grades teacher were working on an activity that could be completed satisfactorily via arithmetic. The teacher saw an opportunity for algebraic thinking and said, "Once you have made a chart, look for an easier way. Pay attention to how the numbers group and how the groupings might suggest an easier way."

- Making it a habit to ask a variety of questions aimed at helping students organize their thinking and respond to algebraic prompts. For example, we have noted among some Linked Learning teachers a consistent use of questions that challenge students to analyze expressions: "Can you explain what the 3 and the 5 represent in that equation?"

We have been paying particular attention to the value of questioning. A couple of beliefs have grown out of the work we have done in our teacher-enhancement projects. One has to do with the role of *intention* in teachers' questioning; the other has to do with the mathematical *context* in which the question is asked:

TABLE 1–1. *Guiding Questions*

Questions for Doing—and Undoing	Questions for Building Rules to Represent Functions	Questions for Abstracting from Computation
How is this number in the sequence related to the one that came before?	Is there a rule or relationship here?	How is this calculating situation like/unlike that one?
What if I start at the end?	How does the rule work, and how is it helpful?	How can I predict what's going to happen without doing all the calculation?
Which process reverses the one I'm using?	Why does the rule work the way it does?	What are my operation shortcut options for getting from here to there?
Can I decompose this number or expression into helpful components?	How are things changing?	When I do the same thing with different numbers, what still holds true? What changes?
	Is there information here that lets me predict what's going to happen?	
	Does my rule work for all cases?	What are other ways to write that expression that will bring out hidden meaning?
	What steps am I doing over and over?	
	Can I write down a mechanical rule that will do this job once and for all?	How can I write the expression in terms of things I care about?
	How can I describe the steps without using specific inputs?	How does this expression behave like that one?
	When I do the same thing with different numbers, what still holds true? What changes?	
	Now that I have an equation, how do the numbers (parameters) in the equation relate to the problem context?	

1. **Intention.** It is valuable for teachers to be aware of the variety and breadth of intention behind classroom questions and to seek, over time, patterns of questioning that are balanced across the range of intention.

2. **Context.** Questions aimed at developing students' algebraic thinking patterns should be asked in situations that are patently "algebraic," as well as in situations in which the relevance of algebraic thinking isn't as obvious.

Ideally, once the teacher is able to concentrate wholly on algebraic thinking, the questions will sound like these adaptations from the questions listed in Table 1–1:

- Which process reverses the one you're using?

- How does the rule work?

- How are things changing?

- Can you find a more helpful way to write the rule?

- Is there information here that lets you predict what's going to happen?

- How can you predict what's going to happen without doing all the calculation?

- What are your operation shortcut options for getting from here to there?

- When you do the same thing with different numbers, what still holds true? What changes?

Of course, teachers in real classrooms are dealing with factors that often make the ideal seem remote and, perhaps, unrealistic. Usually, considerable groundwork must be laid for asking algebraic-thinking questions.

Intention

To get a handle on the kinds of questions that lay this groundwork, the Linked Learning Project relied on a cadre of teacher leaders who act as classroom observers of the project's teachers, and asked them to pay special heed to the questions asked by the teachers and the impact of these questions on students. The observations take place in classes in which the teachers are using a lesson meant to elicit algebraic thinking from the students.[1] In post-observation debriefings, the observer checks with the teacher on the accuracy of the observer's judgment about the intended purpose of each recorded question. From the observation data, we found that teachers' questions fall into five categories, according to a teacher's general intention in asking them (Table 1–2).

Any effective lesson or set of lessons will use a blend of question types. Because students can need clarification on what a mathematical challenge is asking them to do, because their attention may need orienting toward key features, and because their underlying reasoning may not be clear or may seem incomplete or faulty, teachers need to use a variety of questions or prompts that are not particularly algebraic, but that lay groundwork for and, ideally, foreshadow students' algebraic thinking.

Context

In addition to teacher intention, mathematical context is another consideration in teachers' use of classroom questions to elicit algebraic thinking and, over time, to foster the development of algebraic habits of mind. Some of the activities that teachers use will display their algebraic potential rather explicitly. For example, there is a clear call for finding a rule to describe a pattern ("What is a general way

TABLE 1–2. *Five Categories of Teacher's Questions*

Question Type	Examples
Managing Intended to help set students on task, get their work organized, etc.	Who's in charge of writing it down? Are you guys working? What are you doing now?
Clarifying Intended to request information from the student when the teacher isn't clear about what the student means or intends; also, when the teacher is trying to help the student clarify the question	Do you know what *perimeter* is? How did you get 2? (This is asked when the teacher is trying to follow the student's thinking, not trying to correct thinking or help refocus it in a different direction.) Who went first? (during a mathematics game)
Orienting Intended to get students started, or to keep them thinking about the particular problem they are solving; may suggest ways to focus on the problem; also, to orient and/or motivate the student toward the correct answer or away from the incorrect answer	What's the problem asking you to find? Have you thought about trying a table? If you have that number and it increases 3, what do you get? (emphasis on error) How did you get 18 (when the answer is some other value)? How can you check your answer? (wrong answer)
Prompting Mathematical Reflection Intended to ask students to reflect on and explain their thinking; to have them understand others' mathematical ways of thinking; and to have them extend their thinking about the mathematics in a problem	How do you explain that? Can you explain how you got the values in the table? Why did the two of you reach different conclusions? Can you estimate? . . . Now check. Does anyone have a different way?
Eliciting Algebraic Thinking Intended to ask the students to undo, to build rules for describing functional relationships; to abstract from computations they have made; to ask about the meaning of the work they're doing; to ask about what statements are "always" true, about nth terms, and about finding patterns and looking for what changes; to work forward and backward, etc.; and to ask students to justify generalizations	What could it (the value in the equation) represent? How could you use the formula? In x years, how much does it go up? Can you look for a pattern? Find out how the rule works. What does -2 mean? If this is 13 and this is 16, by how much did it increase? (emphasis on change) What is an easier way? Pay attention to how the numbers group.

to say how high the tree will be after n months?"), or students are asked to make a general statement drawn from a particular calculation (e.g., "$5 = 9 - 4$. How many odd numbers can be written as the difference of two perfect squares? Show why you think you have them all."). In such cases, teacher questions can reinforce students' appreciation of what are important features, such as

- comparing the relative value of different representations of a relation: "What does the graph tell you? Now, what different information does the equation give you?"

- looking back, after a solution, for a shortcut that may have been missed and could be useful next time: "How could you have reached that conclusion without looking at the chart?"

- making sure that all the relevant cases have been found: "How can you be sure you have found all the numbers that work?"

- seeing what happens when other numbers are tried: "What if you try a much larger number there?"

In other activities, it is likely that the full algebraic potential—or, in many cases, *any* algebraic potential—will go unexploited unless the teacher asks questions that are used to extend students' thinking about the problem. In those cases, the teacher may be

1. reversing a routine calculating task to challenge students to undo as well as do: "Now that you have a good handle on using a factor tree, answer this: What whole numbers have three factors, including the factor of 1?"

2. asking "what if" questions to extend beyond a single situation to a more generalized situation. For example, suppose students have solved the following problem:

Golden Apples[2]

A prince picked a basketful of golden apples in the enchanted orchard. On his way home, he was stopped by a troll who guarded the orchard. The troll demanded payment of one-half of the apples plus two more. The prince gave him the apples and set off again. A little further on, he was stopped by a second troll guard. This troll demanded payment of one-half of the apples the prince now had plus two more. The prince paid him and set off again. Just before leaving the enchanted orchard, a third troll stopped him and demanded one-half of his remaining apples plus two more. The prince paid him and sadly went home. He had only two golden apples left. How many apples had he picked?

Rather than settle for the solution only, the teacher can further students' thinking by asking, "What if he had 4 left? How many did he begin with? 6 left?", and so on.

3. exploiting calculating situations in which there is regularity, to challenge students to use calculating shortcuts based on the regularity (e.g., "Without writing out all the numbers and adding them, find the total: $1 + 2 + 3 + \ldots + 27 + 28 + 27 + \ldots + 3 + 2 + 1$.")

4. exploiting calculating situations in which there is regularity, to challenge students to make general statements (e.g., "Think of three consecutive integers and multiply them. Does 2 divide any such product? Why? What other integers divide any such product? What is the largest integer that you can be certain divides any such product evenly? Why?")

Analyses of student work can support the use of classroom questions to foster algebraic thinking, in particular, prompting reflections about appropriate questions. For example, consider Figure 1–2, a piece of student work, drawn from a Linked Learning classroom.

After examining the sample in Figure 1–2, ask yourself what you notice and what it makes you wonder about. What do you infer about the student's line of thinking? What is noticed, inferred, or wondered about can lead to productive instructional questions. What questions might you ask in order to help the student push her thinking further?

One feasible inference is that the student is onto something productive in the last answer, something like, "When I divide the number of the square into the number of its toothpicks, I get 4, 6, 8, 10 for the four squares that I have." From a habit-of-mind perspective, it seems that the student has wondered, "How are things changing?"—a key question in Building Rules to Represent Functions. It also seems that she has done some fluid Doing–Undoing to test how 4, 12, 24, and 40 could be generated from, respectively, 1, 2, 3, 4.

The following are questions that might push the student further: "What have you done to get these numbers?" "When you were counting toothpicks, were you using any counting shortcuts?" "What information is here to help you predict what's going to happen in the next squares?" In "later squares?"

Example Activities

In this section, we offer several mathematical activities, which we believe can illustrate some of our points about algebraic thinking and the role of classroom questioning. Furthermore, on the basis of the experience of teachers in our projects, we are confident that these activities can be used with students in grades 6 through 10.

FIGURE 1–2.   *Student Work from a Linked Learning Classroom*

Toothpick Squares   Name _____

Shown below is a pattern of "growing" squares made from toothpicks.

1. Study the pattern and draw a picture of the next likely shape in the pattern.

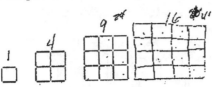

2. How many small squares make up the new square?

16 Small squares

3. How many small squares would make up a large square which has 10
   toothpicks on each side? (Show your work.)   100 square

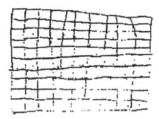

4. Write a rule which will allow you to find the number of small squares in any
   large square.

   1 - 1   8 - 64   they have to time the
   2 · 4   9 - 81   number by it self
   3 - 9   10 - 100
   4 - 16
   5 - 25
   6 - 36
   7 - 119

5. Find a rule which will let you find the number of toothpicks in any large
   square. (Show your work.)

   1 - 4 (4)
   2 - 12 (6)
   3 - 24 (8)
   4 - 40 (10)

The Locker Problem

The potential for algebraic thinking in this problem is substantial but somewhat hidden. At first, and even second, glance, the problem may seem no more than a number-sense problem, involving knowledge about factoring whole numbers.

The Locker Problem[3]

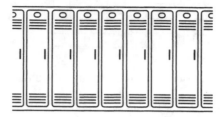

There are 20 lockers in one hallway of the King School. In preparation for the beginning of school, the janitor closed all of the lockers and put a new coat of paint on the doors, which are numbered from 1 to 20.

When the 20 students from Mrs. Mahoney's class returned from summer vacation, they decided to celebrate by working off some energy. They came up with a plan: The first student ran down the row of lockers and opened every door. The second student started with locker #2 and closed every second door. The third student started with locker #3 and changed the state of every third locker door. The fourth student started with locker #4 and changed the state of every fourth locker door, the fifth student started with locker #5 and changed the state of every fifth locker door, and so on, until all 20 students had passed by the lockers.

Which lockers are still open after the twentieth student is finished? Which locker or lockers changed the most?

Suppose there are 200 lockers. Which lockers are open after the 200th student is finished? Which locker or lockers changed the most?

The number of times a locker changes state is the same as the number of factors of the number on the locker: For example, locker number 12 has factors 1, 2, 3, 4, 6, and 12, so it changes state six times. A locker whose number has the most factors is the locker that changes the most. For the 20-locker case, lockers numbered 12, 18, and 20 share this honor. Some students think, by extension, that, for 200 lockers, lockers numbered 120, 180, and 200 change the most. Why would they think this? Why might they be wrong? This starts to get at why we like the potential for algebraic thinking here, because it raises questions about the function whose input is a whole number N and whose output is the number of factors of N. This is usually called the nu function, after the Greek letter ν. Using this terminology, $\nu(12) = 6$. If you sketch the graph of ν, it moves up and down rather wildly. Consequently, you would not expect ν to be describable by any succinct rule. However, it turns out that any whole number N can be factored into its "prime factorization," $p_1^{k_1}, \ldots, p_m^{k_m}$, where $p_1, \ldots, p_m$ are distinct primes and $k_1, \ldots, k_m$ are whole numbers. It is the case that $v(N)$ equals the product of $(k_1 + 1), \ldots, (k_m + 1)$. For example, the prime factorization of 12 is $2^2 3^1$, so the rule says that $v(12)$ should be $(2 + 1)(1 + 1) = 6$, which we already know it is. Why does this formula work for v? Think about how factors of a number are constructed from their prime factors.

A locker is open at the end if it changes state an odd number of times. If you record the numbers between 1 and 200 with an odd number of factors, you get 1, 4, 9, 16, 25, 36, and so on, namely, the perfect squares. Why might this be the case? Thinking about the formula for v can give you an idea.

By now, it should be evident how The Locker problem can elicit algebraic thinking, in particular, the habits of mind Building Rules to Represent Functions (in particular, working to represent v) and Doing–Undoing (addressing reverse questions, such as "What numbers have 6 factors? 3 factors? An odd number of factors?").

Relevant guiding questions, from the list offered earlier:

- Can I write down a mechanical rule that will do this job once and for all?

- How does the rule work, and how is it helpful?

- Why does the rule work the way it does?

- What if I start at the end?

- What process reverses the one I am using?

Crossing the River

This problem has proved to be widely accessible to students in grades 6 through 10. Students can represent the situation in verbal, tabular, pictorial, or symbolic (i.e., with equation) forms.

Crossing the River[4]

Eight adults and two children need to cross a river. A small boat is available that can hold one adult or one or two children (i.e., three possibilities: 1 adult in the boat, 1 child in the boat, or 2 children in the boat). Everyone can row the boat. How many one-way trips does it take for all of them to cross the river? Can you describe how to work it out for 2 children and any number of adults? How does your rule work out for 100 adults?

What happens to the rule if there are different numbers of children? For example: 8 adults and 3 children? 8 adults and 4 children? Write a rule for finding the number of trips needed for A adults and C children.

One group of adults and children took 27 trips. How many adults and children were in the group? Is there more than one solution?

Once you see that the same sequence of 4 trips can be repeated over and over again, you can use this chunk to build a rule, and to extend it to any number of adults with 2 children. Students familiar with algebra may symbolize the chunk of 4 in an equation like $4A + 1$ = number of one-way trips. (Question to consider: If the 4 represents the sequence of trips that gets repeated, what does the 1 represent?) However, they may just as easily represent the chunk pictorially, as did the student who drew Figure 1–3.

The introduction of different numbers of children requires a reworking of the rule. This calls into play several of the guiding questions listed earlier. One thing that changes is the number of trips with no adults in the boat. The repeated sequence of 4 trips per adult does not change. A symbolic way to express the rule for A adults and C children: number of one-way trips = $4A + 2C - 3$. (Question to consider: What does $2C - 3$ represent?)

FIGURE 1–3. *Student Pictorial of Rule*

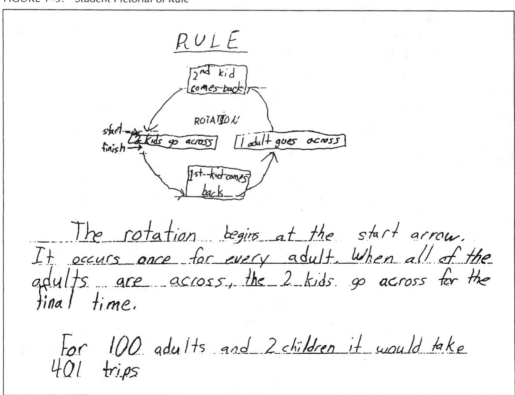

Relevant guiding questions:

- What steps am I doing over and over?

- When I do the same thing with different numbers, what still holds true? What changes?

- Now that I have an equation, how do the numbers (parameters) in the equation relate to the problem context?

Finally, the activity prompts some Doing–Undoing thinking by giving the final state (27 one-way trips) and asking for the starting conditions (i.e., the numbers of children and adults). This tends to be difficult, though not impossible, for middle school students. For more experienced students, it is the kind of situation that shows how powerful algebraic representation can be. For instance, a person who is aware of the $4A + 2C - 3$ expression can use it to work backward from $4A + 2C - 3 = 27$ (or $4A + 2C = 30$). Can you sense, by looking at this, that there is likely to be more than one solution?

Equations such as $4A + 2C = 30$, with integer solutions and integer coefficients, are examples of *Diophantine Equations*, so there are ample extensions to the Crossing the River problem that can spur algebraic thinking.

Cuisenaire Trains

This is an example of an activity that may not look particularly "algebraic" in its context, but it does invite the building of rules to represent functions. It is a rich problem, the solution of which can be obtained by systematically manipulating Cuisenaire rods, recording the results in a two-column table, and looking for patterns.

Cuisenaire Trains[5]

How many Cuisenaire trains can you make, the total length of which is 2? 3? 4? 10? By a "train" of length 3, we mean a row of rods, the length of which is 3, where order counts.

Make a table. Inspection of the table (total length, T, vs. number of trains, N) reveals a doubling pattern that can be expressed symbolically using the equation $N = 2^{T-1}$ (or its recursive version $N_{k+1} = 2N_k$). So, for example, the students can predict that there are $2^{10-1} = 2^9 = 512$ different trains of length 10. One way to justify that there are 2^{T-1} different trains of length T is to think of having a solid rod of length T and a saw to make cuts. For example, for $T = 6$, you have a choice of making a cut, or not, at five different locations; that is, you have 2^5 possible configurations that you can cut with the saw.

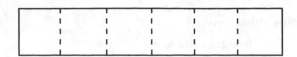

This kind of thinking may be beyond students. Instead, they may justify the doubling by examining the process of making trains of length $T + 1$ from the trains of length T by placing a 1-rod in the front of each train and then a 1-rod at the end of each train. You may want to take a moment now to figure out how close this procedure comes to doubling and what modification needs to be made to reveal the doubling.

For advanced students, further analysis can reveal there are

$$\binom{T-1}{M-1}$$

trains of length T that are composed of M rods. For example, there are

$$\binom{5-1}{3-1} = \binom{4}{2} = 6$$

different trains of length 5 that are composed of 3 rods. They are 122, 212, 221, 113, 131, and 311. Students can justify this result by noting that each of the 6 trains can be thought of as the result of dividing a 5-rod at two of the possible 4-unit lengths. For example, the following diagram shows that the train 122 can be obtained by dividing a 5-rod at the two places indicated by solid lines.

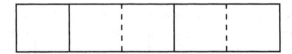

Relevant guiding questions:

- Is there a rule or relationship here?

- How are things changing?

- Is there information here that lets me predict what's going to happen?

- How is this number in the sequence related to the one that came before?

Conclusion

In this chapter and, more broadly, in this book, we advocate for the value of classroom questions in fostering algebraic habits of mind among students in the prealgebra years and beyond. Our framework for shifting classroom practice in this direction isn't based on any attempt to be comprehensive in defining *algebra* or *algebraic thinking*. Rather, it is based on our work with what we believe are three key algebraic habits of mind: Doing–Undoing, Building Rules to Represent Functions, and Abstracting from Computation.

In the following chapters, we address some key issues that arise for teachers in grades 6 through 10 as they try to foster their students' algebraic thinking, in particular, through their classroom questions. The three habits of mind play a key role in our discussions, so we end this chapter with a table for each habit. The information in each table, while not intended to be comprehensive, should provide some concrete examples and connections. Recall what we mean by each of the habits of mind:

- **Doing–Undoing.** Effective algebraic thinking sometimes involves reversibility (i.e., being able to undo mathematical processes as well as do them). In effect, it is the capacity not only to use a process to get to a goal, but also to understand the process well enough to work backward from the answer to the starting point (Table 1–3).

- **Building Rules to Represent Functions.** Critical to algebraic thinking is the capacity to recognize patterns and organize data to represent situations in which input is related to output by well-defined functional rules (Table 1–4).

- **Abstracting from Computation.** This is the capacity to think about computations independently of particular numbers used. One of the most evident characteristics of algebra has always been its abstractness. But, just what is being abstracted? In answer, a good case can be made that thinking algebraically involves being able to think about computations freed from the particular numbers to which they are tied in arithmetic (i.e., abstracting system regularities from computation) (Table 1–5).

Notes

1. Half of the observed lessons in any one teacher's classroom are chosen by the teacher; the other half are activities that are given to the teacher by project staff.
2. From *Make It Simpler*, by Carol Meyer and Tom Sallee; copyright 1983 by Addison–Wesley Publishing Company. Reprinted by permission.
3. This version of the activity was developed by EDC staff for professional development projects. Other versions of the activity can be found in various materials, such as the Grade 6 unit Prime Time, from *Connected Mathematics*. 1998. Menlo Park, CA: Dale Seymour Publications.
4. A similar version of this problem appears in *MathScape: Seeing and Thinking Mathematically, Patterns in Numbers and Shapes, Lesson 3*. 1998. Mountain View, CA: Creative Publications.
5. This version of this problem was developed by Al Cuoco and the EDC staff for EDC professional development projects.

(text continues on page 19)

TABLE 1–3. *Doing–Undoing*

Some Related Mathematical Ideas	Some Possible Indicators	Examples
Inverse Operations; Roots; Functions; Equivalent Expressions This habit of thinking need not wait until the topics of functions or solving equations arise. Throughout the elementary and middle school experiences, there are many topics that provide opportunities to foster a Doing–Undoing habit of mind.	Works to relate one entry to previous entries ("How is this number related to the ones that came before?")	How many even numbers are there in the 100th row of Pascal's Triangle? ("You can build the 100th row from the 99th row—each entry is the sum of the two entries right above it. . . .")
For example, dividing one number into another can result in a remainder. Working backward from remainders can foster student thinking about the process or algorithm used in the dividing.	Deduces input from given output, or estimates input from output ("What if I start at the end?")	How would you describe all the numbers with exactly three factors? ("Well, two of the factors are 1 and the number itself, so what could the third one look like?") In the Locker problem, which locker(s) do you think change states the most? ("I think that the biggest power of 2 less than 200 may be the answer, because it would have a lot of factors. . . .")
	Uses an inverse process (works backward through a sequence of steps) ("What process reverses the one I'm using?")	When my age is divided by 3, the remainder is 1. When my age is divided by 5, the remainder is 3. When my age is divided by 7, the remainder is 1. How old am I? ("First of all, what numbers have a remainder of 1 when divided by 3? . . .") Find a binomial that multiplies by $4x - 3$ to give $16x^2 - 9$. ("Well, $16x^2 - 9$ is the difference of two squares.")

TABLE 1–4. *Building Rules to Represent Functions*

Some Related Mathematical Ideas	Several Possible Indicators	Examples
Patterns; Functions; Relations		
The NCTM Standards refer frequently to the importance of learners having consistent experience with relations, patterns, and functions. These form the content umbrella for this habit of thinking.	Uses repeating "chunks" to build a process for solving a problem ("Is there information here that let's me predict what's going to happen?") ("Am I doing the same steps over and over?")	(In the Crossing the River problem) How many one-way trips are needed if there are A adults and 2 children? ("It takes 4 one-way trips to complete the process of getting one adult across. Repeat this A times, then . . .")
Of particular relevance are input–output approaches of some curriculum materials to the concept of functions, sometimes called a function–machine approach.	Works from a table to develop a general rule and shows how it can generate any table entry ("Is there a rule or relationship here?") ("When I do the same thing with different numbers, what stays the same? What changes?")	How many Cuisenaire trains are there for any length N? ("For a smaller length m, the number of trains is . . . ")
	Describes a sequence of steps taking input to output. ("Can I write down a mechanical rule that will do this job once and for all?")	How many creases will a piece of paper have if you fold it in half n times? ("Each time I fold the paper, what does it do to the existing creases?")

TABLE 1–5. *Abstracting from Computation*

Some Related Mathematical Ideas	Several Indicators	Examples
Integers; Prime Numbers; Properties of Number Systems; Operations; Modular Arithmetic		
There are numerous opportunities before formal algebra to enable learners to abstract from calculation. Young learners are developing this habit of thinking when they are using the fact that multiplication among whole numbers is repeated addition. Later, they may internalize the distributive property in the context of an investigation when one group of students develops a rule, "Add the two numbers and multiply by 3," while another group develops the (equally valid) rule, "Multiply each of the two numbers by 3, then add them." Or, they may wonder whether, when a sum of integers is divided by an integer (call it *m*), the remainder is the sum of the remainders when each of the integers is divided by *m*.	Generalizes, using the relationships among addition, multiplication, subtraction, and division. ("How does this expression behave like that one?")	What whole numbers can be expressed as the sum of five consecutive whole numbers? ("I did it the same way I answered the question about three consecutive numbers. In this case, the number has to be divisible by 5. Take the middle of the five consecutive numbers. The original number is going to be 5 times this, because . . .")
	Uses knowledge of properties to develop shortcuts ("How can I predict without doing all the work?") ("What are my operation shortcut options?")	Compute $1 + 2 + 3 + \ldots + 98 + 99 + 100$ ("I can group in pairs that equal 101: $[1 + 100] + [2 + 99] + [3 + 98] \ldots$")
		Which is greater, 5% of 7 billion dollars or 7% of 5 billion dollars? ("I know that 5% of 7 billion dollars is the same amount as 7% of 5 billion dollars, without computing.")
	Calculates readily with letter symbols, freed from the need to know what the symbols stand for ("How does this expression behave like that expression?") ("What does this have to do with the rules of calculation?")	Investigate and explain this pattern: $1/2 - 1/3 = 1/2 \times 1/3$ $1/3 - 1/4 = 1/3 \times 1/4$ $1/4 - 1/5 = 1/4 \times 1/5$, etc. ("$1/n - 1/[n + 1] = [1/n] \times [1/(n + 1)]$ is true because . . .")
	Using equivalent expressions, simplifying or complicating, depending on need ("What other ways are there to write that expression that will bring out hidden meaning?")	$x^2 - 4 - y^2 + 4$ is simplified to $x^2 - y^2$; alternatively, for certain purposes, $x^2 - y^2$ can be "complicated" to $x^2 - 4 - y^2 + 4$.
	Computes in different systems ("How is this calculating situation like/unlike that one?")	$x^2 + 7x = 0$ has four solutions in the system of integers modulo 10.

References and Further Reading

Bednarz, N. & C. Janvier. 1996. "Emergence and Development of Algebra as a Problem-Solving Tool: Continuities and Discontinuities with Arithmetic." In *Approaches to Algebra: Perspectives for Research and Teaching,* eds. N. Bednarz, C. Kieran & L. Lee, 115–36. Dordrecht, The Netherlands: Kluwer Academic.

Cuoco, A. 1992. *Action to Process: Constructing Functions from Algebra Word Problems.* Newton, MA: Education Development Center.

Davis, B. 1997. "Listening for Differences: An Evolving Conception of Mathematics Teaching." *Journal for Research in Mathematics Education* 28: 355–76.

Driscoll, M., J. Moyer & J. Zawojewski. "Helping Teachers Implement Algebra for All in Milwaukee Public Schools." *Mathematics Education Leadership* 2: 3–12.

Langrall, C.W. & J.O. Swafford. 1997. "Grade Six Students' Use of Equations to Describe and Represent Problem Situations." Paper presented at the annual meeting of the American Educational Research Association, Chicago, Illinois, March 1997.

Meyer, C. & T. Sallee. 1983. *Make It Simpler: A Practical Guide to Problem Solving in Mathematics.* Menlo Park, CA: Addison Wesley.

Smith, J.P. III. 1996. "Efficacy and Teaching Mathematics by Telling: A Challenge for Reform." *Journal for Research in Mathematics Education Reform* 27: 387–402.

2 Smoothing the Transition to Algebra Through Algorithmic Thinking

Algorithms and Algebraic Thinking

School algebra has earned a reputation as mysterious and intimidating because it is often presented to students in ways that bear little connection to the "math" they have done in previous years. Typically, students reach ninth or tenth grade and all those years of computing with numbers to get numerical answers are replaced by a new set of experiences, characterized by their reliance on letter symbols, not numbers, and by a set of arcane rules for manipulating these symbols. To add to the mystery and intimidation, often those manipulations are not carried out to yield a numerical answer. Various confusions and distractions can arise for students. For example, the fact that the expressions $4x + 8$ and $4(x + 2)$ are equivalent might be lost on students distracted by wondering about the numerical value of $4x + 8$.

Another transitional rough spot for students is a subtle but significant shift in perspective on the *role* of computations. In using arithmetic, students typically work through a string of computations to get to a desired goal. Strings that are used again and again, recipe-like, are given names like "division algorithm" and "multiplication algorithm," wherein *algorithm* means a description of a mechanical set of steps for performing some task. While some standard computing algorithms, like the division and multiplication algorithms, have places in arithmetic, others have places in other areas of mathematics, such as geometry and number theory. For example, geometry is replete with algorithms for calculating things such as the area and perimeter of a figure, and number theory has many algorithms, such as the factor-tree algorithm.

Even when students are using a computational algorithm again and again, they likely experience the different steps of the algorithm as separate actions. Nothing in arithmetic demands that they do otherwise; however, things change in algebra. For example, Cuoco (1992) has written about the very different ways in which the following two word problems are experienced by learners (3):

1. Debbie bought 36 apples at 25 cents each. She ate 2 of them, and she sold the rest for 32 cents each. What was her profit?

2. Debbie bought some apples at 25 cents each. She ate 2 of them, and she sold the rest for 32 cents each. If her profit was $1.88, how many apples did she buy?

The first, a typical prealgebra word problem, can be done with a straightforward string of computational actions: subtract 2 from 36; multiply the answer by 32; from that number subtract the product of 25 and 36. Students often think of each of these computational steps as its own independent action and do not think about the string of steps as a whole entity that takes input and yields output. In contrast, in the second word problem, typical of algebra, students are given output and then asked to find input. This kind of challenge demands a different way of thinking about and dealing with the calculations used: To map back from output to input, students must think in terms of *functions* that yield output from input, and they must find a way to package calculations together to form the appropriate function. In this case, the function takes given input, subtracts 2 from it, multiplies the result by 32, and then subtracts from this result the result of multiplying the input by 25. Knowing the output is 188 allows one to reason back to the input. In essence, this is a significant shift because it demands that students start thinking of a computation-based algorithm not as a string of independent actions, but as a process, an entity unto itself.

In recent years, classroom materials to support students in the transition from arithmetic to algebra have become available; in particular, several comprehensive K through 4 and 5 through 8 curriculum projects have undertaken to foreshadow formal algebra regularly in their lessons. For the materials to be effective, however, it is important that teachers adopt a developmental, cross-grades perspective on algebraic thinking. In the context of the current chapter, this means that teachers need to be alert for threads of student thinking that are rule-driven and based on the inclination students develop to use step-by-step computational procedures. These threads of student thinking are important because they signal opportunities to shift student attention from individual computational actions to the whole procedure encompassing the actions. In doing this, students develop habits of thinking in terms of algorithmic and functional processes.

Finding Algebraic Potential in Unexpected Places

Many view algebra as having rather rigid boundaries; they see algebra as rule-based manipulation of symbols to model problems and solve equations. However, algebraic boundaries are permeable, and algebraic habits of mind can appear in a variety of settings. It is important that teachers be alert to finding algebraic thinking in ostensibly nonalgebraic settings.

Opportunities to develop students' algorithmic thinking arise in unexpected places. After working on the following problem in small groups, teachers from one of our projects became involved in an interesting discussion about the boundaries of algebra and algorithmic thinking in the problem. (This problem was discussed briefly in Chapter 1.)

Golden Apples[1]

A prince picked a basketful of golden apples in the enchanted orchard. On his way home, he was stopped by a troll who guarded the orchard. The troll demanded payment of one-half of the apples plus two more. The prince gave him the apples and set off again. A little further on, he was stopped by a second troll guard. This troll demanded payment of one-half of the apples the prince now had plus two more. The prince paid him and set off again. Just before leaving the enchanted orchard, a third troll stopped him and demanded one-half of his remaining apples plus two more. The prince paid him and sadly went home. He had only two golden apples left. How many apples had he picked?

→Before reading on, work through the problem. Pay attention to how you are thinking about it—where you start, planned steps, and so on.

By revealing the output and asking for the input, the problem is structured to underscore the relevance of algorithmic thinking to algebra. And, in fact, after the teachers worked on the Golden Apples problem in small groups, their reporting back to the full group was replete with careful step-by-step procedures that worked backward from the given data. For example,

1. $x/2 - 2$,   remainder after first troll toll

2. $1/2[x/2 - 2] - 2$,   remainder after second troll toll

3. $1/2[1/2[x/2 - 2] - 2] - 2$,   remainder after third troll toll

4. $1/2[1/2[x/2 - 2] - 2] - 2 = 2$

5. $1/2[1/2[x/2 - 2] - 2] = 4$

6. $1/2[x/2 - 2] - 2 = 8$, etc., to

   $x = 44$

One of the sixth-grade teachers in the group, Albert, spoke up: "I'd let my students approach this with guess-and-check. You know what I mean? Let them try a number, say 60. They run it through and, since we know the answer is 44, they'd find it leaves too many apples, so I'd ask, 'Okay, if 60 gives a number too large, what number would make more sense to try next?'"

Albert's remark was greeted with general agreement from around the room. There was no question that guess-and-check seemed a fair alternative, in this case, to the more symbolic, "algebraic" approach, especially since it would offer access to students with no algebra background. However, there was a question worth considering here: To what extent is there a real difference between the symbolic approach and Albert's students' guess-and-check? Is one viewed as "algebra" and the other as something else, but not algebra?

We believe that the boundaries in the meanings attached to "algebraic think-ing" should be more permeable. In particular, we think that building equations using symbols and applying guess-and-check are both representative of the habit of mind we call Building Rules to Represent Functions (see Chapter 1).

Let's look for a minute at why guess-and-check can work for the Golden Apples problem. Albert said that he'd ask students to pick a starting number. Put yourself in the students' shoes and consider the following questions:

- Is any starting number as good as any other? Some starting numbers, in fact, lead to answers that are not whole numbers. Albert picked 60, and that led to a whole number. Was that luck? Or was he implicitly applying something that he had noticed about the numbers?

- What information about the numbers in the problem can help in choosing a starting number that leads to a whole number answer? In fact, what are the starting numbers that lead to whole numbers? They are the numbers 36, 44, 52, 60, and so on, right? What does that tell you?

- When Albert asks his students, "What would make sense to try next?" what will determine what "makes sense?" Using 60 as a starting number would leave 4 at the end. We want an output of 2. Do we try a number larger than 60, or smaller? Why?

In your answers to these questions, you might have thought of the terms *in-creasing linear function* and *slope of 1/8*. However, even if you didn't, it is likely that you were aware of responding to a gut sense about order and predictability and asking yourself a variety of questions, such as the following ones:

- Is there information here that lets me predict what's going to happen?

- How are things changing?

- When I do the same thing with different numbers, what still holds true? What changes?

It also is likely that you were thinking in terms of input and output, one of the hallmarks of computational algorithms and the basis of many of the functions fea-tured in formal algebra. In any event, you were engaging in very productive, if not explicit, algebraic thinking.

The thinkers in the Golden Apples problem who laid out a procedure with expressions were thinking in the same terms but likely were also asking themselves questions such as the following:

- Can I write down a mechanical rule that will do this job once and for all?

- How can I describe the steps without using specific inputs?

All such considerations are critical to effective algebraic thinking: learning to build mechanical rules that can solve problems efficiently and accurately, but keeping in mind the features of the functions associated with the rules.

Rule-driven, algorithmic thinking is sometimes implicit, as in guess-and-check, and sometimes explicit, as in the equation-building approach. Teachers can help students make the transition to algebra smoother by highlighting not only explicit algorithmic thinking, but also the more implicit algorithmic thinking.

Variety of Algorithmic Thinking

Within single problems, there is often a multiplicity of possible approaches that algorithmic thinkers might take. Teachers can capitalize on these diverse approaches by highlighting each and comparing them with one another. For example, the following activity can elicit from students several different algorithmic approaches to finding a solution to the problem:

Postage Stamp Problem[2]

The post office only has stamps of the denominations 5 cents and 7 cents. What amounts of postage can you buy? Explain your conclusion. What if the denominations are 3 cents and 5 cents? 15 cents and 18 cents?

What generalizations can you make for stamp denominations m cents and n cents, where m and n are positive integers?

→Work on the problem. Before you start: What are you wondering about? Do you have any conjectures? Take special note of your starting point, strategies, and the generalizations you make.

Teachers involved in one of our projects worked on this activity in small groups made up of middle and high school teachers. After a period of time, the groups were asked to report on their progress. The reports (Figure 2–1) encompassed a variety of approaches, each bearing its own distinctive markings of algebraic thinking. In particular, there were several very different slants on Building Rules to Represent Functions. For example, one group showed its work on the first part of the task.

Their approach was to generate tables for each of the three combinations mentioned in the statement of the problem. Each table was an ordered representation of the different combinations of denominations. They recorded enough data to see some patterns emerging. It was easy to infer from the report of their work that the following guiding questions were not too far below the surface:

• Is there information here that lets me predict what's going to happen?

FIGURE 2–1.   *Report on the Postage Stamp Problem*

①

5x+7y	0	1	2	3	4	5	6	7	8	9	10	···	x	
0	0	5	10	15	20	25	30	35	40	45	50		5x	
1	7	12	17	22	27	32	37	42	47	52	57		5x+2	
2	14	19	24	29	34	39	44						5x−1	
3	21	26	31	36	41	46	51	···					5x+1	
4	28	33	38	····									5x+3	
5	35	40	45	50	···								5x	
6	42												5x+2	R
7	49												5x−1	
8	56												5x+1	

②

5x+3y	0	1	2	3	4	5	6	7	···	★	
0	0	3	6	9	12	15	18	21	···	3y	3y
1	5	8	11	14	17	20	23	···			3y+2
2	10	13	16	19	22	25	28	31	···		3y+1
3	15	18	21	24	27	30	33	36	····		3y
4	20	23									3y+2
5	25										3y+1
6	30										
7	35										

③

	0	1	2	3	4	5	6	7		
0	0	15	30	45	60	75	90	105		15x
1	18	33	48	63	78	93	108	123		15x+3
2	36	51	66	81						15x+6
3	54									15x+9
4	72									15x−3
5	90									15x
6	108									

- Is something repeating? Am I doing the same steps over and over? What are they?

- How are things changing?

In the end, they looked at the evidence they had—that in the first two cases (the 3-cent and 5-cent case and the 5-cent and 7-cent case), they had no gaps in the amount of postage after a certain point, while in the last case (the 15-cent and 18-cent case), they had consistent gaps. They conjectured first that they likely could generate *all* the postage beyond those certain points for the first two cases and that, in the general case, the concept "relatively prime" is a key differentiating factor for determining how much postage can be generated by two denominations.

Another group took an entirely different approach. Aiming more at the generalization prompted by the second part of the task, they developed an algorithm with a strong computational flavor. Rather than generate postage combinations to see what combinations were possible, they worked in reverse, starting with an amount of money and finding a condition under which a linear combination of two denominations (such as two 5-cent stamps plus three 7-cent stamps) could equal that amount. They came up with the following conclusion:

> Given an amount of money, A, we divide it by the smaller denomination. If the remainder is divisible by the difference between the denominations, then we know we can generate the combination by using the given denominations. Example: With 5-cent and 7-cent denominations: Try 129. 129 divided by 5 leaves the remainder 4. 4 is divisible by 2, the difference between 7 and 5. So 129 works $[(5 \times 23) + (7 \times 2) = 129]$.

This group's algorithmic thinking seemed to be guided by different questions:

- Can I write down a mechanical rule that will do this job once and for all?

- How can I describe the steps without using specific inputs?

- When I do the same thing with different numbers, what still holds true? What changes?

The two groups approached the underlying algorithm in two fundamentally different ways. To characterize the amounts of postage that can be purchased with two given stamp denominations, the first group generated possible amounts, noticed patterns in the numbers, and came up with a conclusion. The second group took a very different approach: They attempted to come up with a way to characterize possible amounts by examining the structure of those amounts. Both were thinking algorithmically in valuable ways. By encouraging, highlighting, and comparing different ways of approaching problems algorithmically, teachers can help students gain a wider sense of the essence of algorithms and algorithmic thinking.

Guiding question

- What questions might you ask to help students make connections between these two different approaches?

Recommendations for Ongoing Attention to Algorithmic Thinking

As discussed, teachers can help students make the transition to algebra smoother by being aware of opportunities to emphasize algorithmic thinking in ostensibly nonalgebraic contexts and by looking for multiple ways of thinking about problems algorithmically. But, there are also many other ways in which teachers can support the development of algorithmic thinking in their students on an everyday basis. Following are some recommendations:

FIGURE 2–2. *Student's Work on Sums of Consecutive Numbers*

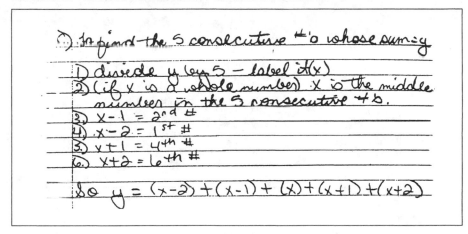

• Look for algorithmic thinking in ostensibly nonalgebraic contexts. As was discussed earlier in the chapter, opportunities for engagement with algorithms can arise in contexts (e.g., guess-and-check) that do not at first seem to be algebraic.

• Highlight and compare different algorithms. Often it is useful to compare different approaches to the same problem, as was discussed earlier in the chapter with the Postage Stamp problem. Sums of Consecutive Numbers is another problem that invites the development of different kinds of algorithms (see the Example Activities section of this chapter).

Figures 2–2 and 2–3 show portions of two students' work on Sums of Consecutive Numbers. In Figure 2–2, the student demonstrates a rule that shows how to take any input number and find the five consecutive numbers whose sum is that number.

Questions that were likely guiding this student include variations on the following:

• What steps am I doing over and over?

• What are other ways to write this expression that will bring out hidden meaning?

• How can I describe the steps without using specific inputs?

The student's work in Figure 2–3 displays rule-based thinking rooted in number theory more than arithmetic. Apparently considering all of the sums of consecutive numbers he or she generated, the student states a relation between the number of factors of an input number and the number of ways that the input number can be represented as a sum of consecutive numbers.

FIGURE 2–3.   *Student's Work on Sums of Consecutive Numbers*

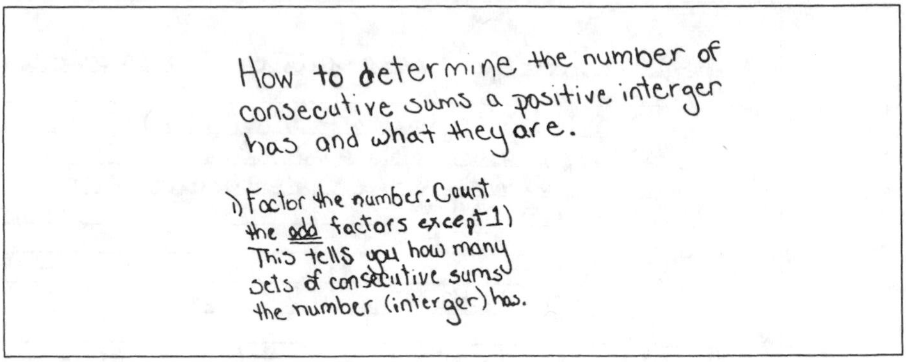

> How to determine the number of consecutive sums a positive interger has and what they are.
>
> 1) Factor the number. Count the <u>odd</u> factors except 1) This tells you how many sets of consecutive sums the number (interger) has.

Guiding questions this student was likely asking include versions of the following:

- Is there a rule or relationship here?

- Can I decompose this number or expression into helpful components?

- When I do the same thing with different numbers, what still holds true? What changes?

Like the two algorithms developed to answer the Postage Stamp problem, these two algorithms represent fundamentally different approaches to the same problem: The first student's algorithm can be used to determine whether a number can be represented as the sum of five consecutive numbers, whereas the second student's algorithm addresses the larger issue of determining the number of ways a given number can be represented as a sum of consecutive numbers. Questions that can help to spur a fruitful conversation about the two algorithms include the following: How are these two algorithms similar or different? What are the advantages and disadvantages that go along with using each algorithm? What questions can and cannot be answered with each algorithm? How are the two algorithms related?

- Look for opportunities for students to describe and explain the algorithms they build. For example, what questions might you ask the students whose work on Sums of Consecutive Numbers is shown in Figures 2–2 and 2–3? Questions such as the following demand that students explain how they developed their algorithm and why their algorithm works:

Questions for Student 1

- Can you use this rule to find five consecutive numbers whose sum is 24?

- Does your rule work for any value of y?

- Why does your rule work?

- How did you come up with your rule?

- How can you be sure that it works?

- Why do you count only the odd factors?

- How many ways can 33 be represented as a sum of consecutive numbers? Show each way 33 can be represented as a sum of consecutive numbers.

Analyzing either student's algorithm can be a springboard for rich discussions about the underlying mathematics.

- Consider whether an activity can be enhanced by using the notion of an input–output machine to represent the steps of an algorithm. Input–output machines help students to see algorithms as single entities that transform input into output. Simultaneously, they help to elucidate specific algorithms by laying out the steps in discrete units. For example, the following input–output machine can help students with the Golden Apples problem:

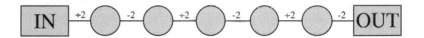

- Incorporate an undoing step to enhance a problem: Give students the output and ask for the input. In the Golden Apples algorithm, suppose there were 6 apples left. How many apples were there to begin with?

- Capitalize on opportunities for students to understand *why* particular computational algorithms work, as well as *when* they work. Students will benefit from figuring out why both standard and alternative computational algorithms work. To see an example of a problem that presents an alternative algorithm for a basic arithmetic operation and asks students to explain why it works, see the Gum problem in the Example Activities section of this chapter.

- Give input and output and ask students to fill in the steps of the algorithm. This is the kind of activity often called "Guess My Rule." The What's My Formula? problem in the Example Activities section of this chapter is a version of this kind of problem, which utilizes spreadsheet software.

- Ask students to identify equivalent algorithms. For example, what could replace the question marks in the following diagram (each question mark may represent a different action):

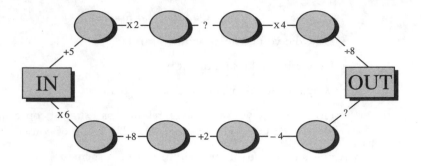

- Seek opportunities for students to extend to other settings algorithms that are associated with arithmetic and number theory. By doing this, students must focus on essential elements of the algorithm in question. For example, see the Algorithm Extensions problem in the Example Activities section of this chapter.

- Provide chances for students to see and develop algorithms that are not computationally based. The Crossing the River activity from the previous chapter is one such example, as the pictorial representation in Figure 2–4 (a student example), also shown in the previous chapter, shows. See also The Cutting Edge and Lots of Squares problems in the Example Activities section of this chapter.

FIGURE 2–4. *Student Pictorial of Rule*

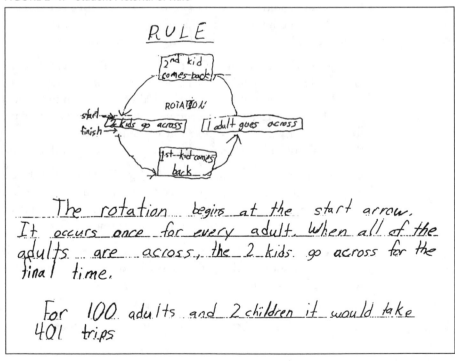

Example Activities

Following are several activities that we believe can invite reflections about the role of algorithms in algebraic thinking. Each problem is followed by a discussion of the problem, including hints or solutions.

A Crawling Snail

This problem requires that students come up with a rule or algorithm; in so doing, it allows for multiple approaches to finding a rule. Some students may want to make tables and come up with a formula from the tables, while others will visualize the situation and reason their way to an algorithm for the general case without the use of a table.

A Crawling Snail[3]

A snail crawling up a pole 5 feet in length went up 4 feet each day and slid back 3 feet each night. How long would the snail take to go to the top? What if the pole were 7 feet in length? 28 feet? *m* feet?

Associated guiding questions:

- Is there a rule or relationship here?
- How are things changing?
- What steps am I doing over and over again?
- When I do the same thing with different numbers, what still holds true? What changes?

Like the Crossing the River problem (see Chapter 1), this problem hinges on the ability to chunk steps. Questions that can help include the following: What is the highest point the snail reaches every day? What is the net distance covered by the snail in any 24-hour period?

Students should eventually find that it takes the snail $m - 3$ days to make it to the top of a pole of length m. This problem has several good extension questions: What if the length of the pole is not an integer? What if the snail moves up *4 feet* every day and slips back *2 feet* every night? What if the snail moves up k feet every day and slips back n feet at night?

Cutting Through the Layers

This problem adds an extra twist to students' thinking about algorithms by dealing with an algorithm that has *two* input values but only one output value. Furthermore, this problem makes a good bridge between the arithmetical notion of algorithm and the algebraic notion because it highlights both the concept of algorithm as entity unto itself and the concept of algorithm as sequence of steps.

Cutting Through the Layers[4]

Imagine a single piece of string, which can be bent back and forth. In the picture below, the string is bent so that it has three "layers."

But it is still one piece of string. Imagine now that you take scissors and cut across the bent string, as indicated by the dotted line. The result will be four separate pieces of string, as shown below.

You could have made more than one cut across the bent string, creating more pieces. In the picture below, two cuts have been made, creating a total of seven pieces.

You could also start with more layers in the bent string. In the picture below, there are four layers and three cuts.

That creates a total of 13 pieces. All of this information about layers, cuts, and pieces of string has been organized into the In–Out table below. Since the number of pieces depends on both the numbers of layers and the number of cuts, there are two inputs, while the number of pieces is the output.

Inputs		Output
Number of Layers	Number of Cuts	Number of Pieces
3	0	1
3	1	4
3	2	7
4	3	13

Make your own pictures of string with different numbers of layers and different numbers of cuts. Count the pieces and add that information to the In–Out table. Now suppose that the number of layers is L and the number of cuts is C. Find a rule or formula expressing the number of pieces as a function of both L and C. In other words, tell what to do with L and C to find out how many pieces there will be.

Associated guiding questions:

- How are things changing?
- What steps am I doing over and over again?
- Now that I've found the rule, how do the numbers (parameters) in the equation relate to the problem context?

This problem is most easily approached by isolating variables. If the number of cuts remains constant, how does the number of pieces vary with the number of bends? If the number of bends remains constant, how does the number of pieces vary with the number of cuts? How can this information be combined into a single rule?

There will be $CL + 1$ pieces of a string with L layers and C cuts. In Chapters 6 and 7, we emphasize the importance of symbol sense and the ability to represent situations in a variety of contexts. One way in which this can be done is by explicitly asking students to relate rules written with symbols to the original context of the problem. Here, students can do this by explaining why $CL + 1$ is the number of pieces of string in terms of the visual image of the string. Questions that might help: What does the "+ 1" mean? How does the number of pieces change after each cut?

Age Problem

The Age problem involves the concept of division remainder. It requires reverse thinking about the process through which remainders arise.

Age Problem[5]

1. Classify all numbers that leave a remainder of 3 when divided by 5 *and* a remainder of 1 when divided by 3.

2. If my age is divided by 3, the remainder is 2. If my age is divided by 5, the remainder is also 2. If my age is divided by 7, the remainder is 5. How old am I?

Associated guiding questions:

- What process reverses the one I'm using?
- When I do the same thing with different numbers, what still holds true? What changes?

1. Questions that might help get into this problem include the following: What are some numbers that leave a remainder of 3 when divided by 5? If I gave you a number that left a remainder of 3 when divided by 5, could you use that number to give me another such number? Can you classify all numbers that leave a remainder of 3 when divided by 5? The set of numbers that leave a remainder of 3 when divided by 5 is $\{3, 8, 13, 18, \ldots\}$—every fifth number beginning at 3. Likewise, the set of numbers that leave a remainder of 1 when divided by 3 is $\{1, 4, 7, 10, \ldots\}$—every third number beginning at 1. By comparing the two sets of numbers, it becomes clear that the set of numbers in both of these sets is $\{13, 28, 43, 58, \ldots\}$—every fifteenth number beginning at 13. Why is this the case? This problem can be extended by examining the same problem with different numbers and looking for general rules. What happens if you leave the numbers by which you divide the *same* and change the numbers that are the *remainders*? What happens if you change the numbers by which you *divide*?

2. Ideas used to solve the first problem can be used to solve this problem. Begin by focusing on the first two constraints on the age in question. Reasoning from the first problem can be applied to this problem to get an age that meets the requirements of the first two constraints is of the form $15x + 2$; in other words, the valid ages must leave a remainder of 2 when divided by 15. Now complete the problem by determining the numbers that leave both a remainder of 2 when divided by 15 and a remainder of 5 when divided by 7. The numbers that fit this description are of the form $105x + 47$. What must the age be?

Sneaking Up the Line

This activity requires building an algorithm based on an understanding of division remainders. The resulting functional relation is an unfamiliar one for middle and even high school students.

Sneaking Up the Line[6]

Eric the Sheep is at the end of a line of 50 sheep waiting to be shorn. But being an impatient sort of a sheep, Eric sneaks up the line two places every time the shearer takes a sheep from the front to be shorn. So, for example, while the first sheep is being shorn, Eric moves ahead so that there are two sheep behind him in line. If at some point it is possible for Eric to move only one place, he does that instead of moving ahead two places.

How many sheep get shorn before Eric?

1. Predict a solution "in your head."

2. Use manipulatives or anything else to solve these two problems:

Number in front of Eric	6	11
Number shorn before Eric		

3. What pattern did you notice that could help you solve the original problem in which Eric is at the end of a line of 50 sheep?

4. Explore other numbers and put the results into a table.

Number in front of Eric							
Number shorn before Eric							

5. Describe how you could work out the answer for any number of sheep.

6. Work out the solutions for the boxes left blank.

Number in front of Eric	37	296	1000			7695
Number shorn before Eric				13	21	

7. Eric gets more (and more) impatient! Explore how your rule changes if Eric sneaks past 3 at a time, 4 at a time, or even 10 at a time. As soon as someone tells you how many sheep are in front of Eric and how many he sneaks past at a time, describe how you could work out the answer.

Associated guiding questions:

- How does the rule work?

- Can I write down a mechanical rule that will do this job once and for all?

- Now that I've found my rule, how do the numbers (parameters) in the equation relate to the problem context?

This problem can be challenging because the underlying function, a step function, is one with which many people are not familiar. Building a table to represent the relation can help to build the rule:

Number of Sheep in Front of Eric	Number of Sheep Shorn Before Eric
1	1
2	1
3	1
4	2
5	2
6	2
7	3
8	3
9	3

Then, questions can help: What patterns do you notice in the right-hand column? What are other ways you might represent this information?

Although discovering this pattern is feasible, many students will struggle to find a way to describe it in functional terms. In the end, students should get an answer equivalent to the following: If the number of sheep in front of Eric is n, then the number of sheep shorn before Eric is $\lceil n/3 \rceil$. (Recall that $\lceil x \rceil$ denotes the smallest integer greater than or equal to x; this function is often called the ceiling function.) For the general case, if Eric sneaks ahead k places, the number of sheep shorn before Eric is $\lceil n/k \rceil$.

Extension Questions: What if the farmer hires another shearer? Suppose there is still one line, but the first and second sheep get shorn at the same time, and then Eric sneaks ahead. What does this do to your rule?

Sums of Consecutive Numbers

As demonstrated by the two pieces of student work in the previous section, this problem can elicit from students algorithms of varying complexity. In addition, it calls on students to use all three habits of mind: Doing–Undoing, Building Rules to Represent Functions, and Abstracting from Computation.

Sums of Consecutive Numbers[7]
$$3 + 4 = 7$$

$$2 + 3 + 4 = 9$$

$$4 + 5 + 6 + 7 = 22$$

These problems are examples of sums of consecutive numbers. The number 7 is shown as the sum of two consecutive numbers. The number 9 is shown as the sum of three consecutive numbers. The number 22 is shown as the sum of four consecutive numbers. In this activity, you will explore what numbers can and cannot be made by sums of consecutive numbers.

1. For each number from 1 to 35, find all the ways to write it as a sum of two or more consecutive numbers.

2. What can you discover about sums of consecutive numbers? Explore and record three discoveries that you can share with the class.

3. Without doing any calculations, predict whether each of the following numbers can be made with 2 consecutive numbers, 3 consecutive numbers, 4 consecutive numbers, and so on. Explain why you made these predictions.

   a.   45

   b.   57

   c.   62

   d.   75

   e.   80

4. Use the discoveries you made in question 2 to come up with shortcuts for writing the following numbers as the sum of two or more consecutive numbers. Describe the shortcuts you created and tell how you used them to write each of the numbers below as sums of consecutive numbers.

   a.   45

   b.   57

   c.   62

   d.   75

   e.   80

Associated guiding questions:

- How is this calculating situation like/unlike that one?
- What are my operation shortcuts for going from here to there?
- How can I write the expression in terms of things I care about?

- How are things changing?

- Can I write down a mechanical rule that will do this job once and for all?

- Can I decompose this number or expression into helpful components?

By capitalizing on regularities in the number system, students can find operation shortcuts that help in this problem. For instance, to calculate $3 + 4 + 5 + 6 + 7$, it is possible to rewrite the sum as $(5 - 2) + (5 - 1) + 5 + (5 + 1) + (5 + 2)$. This simplifies the calculation considerably; the sum is clearly equal to 5×5.

Figuring out whether a given number can be written as the sum of n numbers is relatively straightforward when n is odd. Using reasoning similar to that used above, it is possible to show that, with a few exceptions, if n is an odd factor of a number x, then x can be written as the sum of n consecutive numbers, as follows: $[x/n - (n - 1)/2] + \ldots + (x/n - 2) + (x/n - 1) + x/n + (x/n + 1) + (x/n + 2) + \ldots + [x/n + (n - 1)/2]$. What are the exceptions?

What about when n is even? Think about how you might use a similar strategy to simplify the calculation when n is even. For example, consider the following sum: $5 + 6 + 7 + 8$. This sum could be rewritten as follows: $(6 - 1) + 6 + (6 + 1) + (6 + 2)$. Writing the sum this way highlights that the sum is equal to $4 \times 6 + 2$. Alternatively, the sum could be rewritten in terms of the number halfway between 6 and 7, the number 6.5. Then the sum becomes $(6.5 - 1.5) + (6.5 - 0.5) + (6.5 + 0.5) + (6.5 + 1.5)$. Writing the sum this way points to a different way to calculate the sum: The sum is equal to 4×6.5 or 2×13. What are other ways to write the expression that will bring out hidden meaning?

Think about these two representations. How might you use them to figure out when a given number can be written as the sum of n numbers, where n is even? The problem brings into play Doing–Undoing, in that it requires you to decide, for a given number, whether and how it can be decomposed into a sum of consecutive numbers.

The Cutting Edge

This problem, set in a geometry context, gives students opportunities to work with algorithms that are not number related, thus giving them a better understanding of the concept of algorithm.

The Cutting Edge[8]

Describe an algorithm for cutting up a parallelogram into a rectangle—that is, cutting a parallelogram so that the pieces can be reassembled to form a rectangle. What is an algorithm for cutting up a triangle to form a rectangle?

Associated guiding questions:

- Is there information here that lets me predict what's going to happen?
- Can I write down a mechanical rule that will do this job once and for all?
- Does my rule work for all cases?

Questions that help to get into this problem include the following: What do you know about parallelograms that might help you with this question? How might you use what you know about parallelograms to construct a rectangle from the parallelogram? Because the area of a parallelogram of length l and height h is equal to lh, it is natural to want to transform the parallelogram into a rectangle with length l and height h. One way to think of a parallelogram is as a rectangle with two triangles on either side. One possible algorithm for cutting a parallelogram into a rectangle is to cut off one of the triangles and join it with the other triangle in the appropriate way to make a rectangle.

Cutting up a triangle to form a rectangle is more challenging. The following is one possible answer:

1. Call the triangle ABC. Find the midpoints of AC and BC.

2. Cut from one midpoint to the other. You are now left with a triangle and a trapezoid.

3. Call the midpoint of AC M. Join the triangle and the trapezoid so that MC matches up with AM. You now have a parallelogram.

Lots of Squares

Another problem that asks students to come up with a noncomputational algorithm, Lots of Squares, also invites students to "chunk" steps in order to build their rule.

Lots of Squares[9]

Can you divide a square into a certain number of smaller squares? This may depend on exactly how many smaller squares you want. The first diagram below shows that any square can be divided into 4 smaller squares. The second diagram shows that any square can be divided into 7 smaller squares.

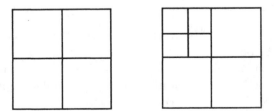

Notice that these smaller squares don't have to be the same size as each other, but keep in mind that the smaller portions must all be squares, not simply rectangles. The task of this activity is to investigate what numbers of smaller squares are possible. For example, you can probably see that there is no way to divide a square into just 2 smaller squares. (Try it and convince yourself that it's impossible.)

1. Start with specific cases. Is it possible to divide a square into 3 smaller squares? 5? 6? 8? (The cases of 4 and 7 smaller squares are shown in the diagrams, although you may want to look for other ways to do them.) Continue this process, at least up to the case of 13 smaller squares.

   Now reflect on what you've done, and just *imagine* continuing this process. Would there be any numbers beyond 13 for which you *couldn't* divide a square into that many smaller squares? What patterns can you find in the cases you've done that help with this question?

2. a. What is the largest "impossible" case?

   b. Prove your answer to question 2a. That is, prove that all cases beyond the one you named in question 2a are possible.

Associated guiding questions:

- Is there a rule or relationship here?
- What steps am I doing over and over?
- Can I write down a mechanical rule that will do this job once and for all?

It is impossible to construct squares with 3 or 5 smaller squares inside of them. Why? The following diagrams demonstrate that it is possible to construct squares with 6 and 8 squares inside of them.

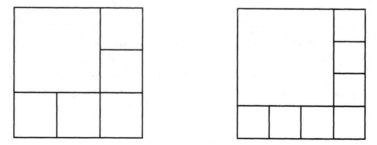

It is also possible to construct squares with 9 to 13 squares inside of them. How can this be done?

Students should eventually find that they can construct squares with any number (except 2, 3, and 5) of subsquares. One possible algorithm they might come up with to construct a square with n subsquares (where n is greater than or equal to 9) is the following:

1. Let y be the remainder of n when divided by 3.

2. If $y = 0$, start with the square with 6 subsquares. Divide one of the subsquares into 4 subsquares, using the division described in the statement of the problem. Now there are 9 squares. Continue dividing squares like this until you have the proper number of subsquares.

3. If $y = 1$, start with the square with 4 subsquares. Divide one of the subsquares into 4 subsquares. Now you have 7 squares. Continue dividing squares like this until you have the proper number of subsquares.

4. If $y = 2$, start with the square with 8 subsquares. Divide one of the subsquares into 4 subsquares. Now you have 11 subsquares. Continue dividing squares like this until you have the proper number of subsquares.

What's My Formula?

By giving students only the inputs and corresponding outputs of a function, this problem emphasizes the idea that algorithms, formulas, and functions can be viewed as entities unto themselves. Additionally, this problem can be an excellent introduction to or reinforcement of the concept of equivalent expressions.

What's My Formula?[10]

You and your partner will need a computer that can produce a spreadsheet for this activity. Player A will make formulas, and Player B will guess hidden formulas. Decide who will be Players A and B. Players switch roles after several rounds. Create a new spreadsheet on your computer. While Player B's eyes are closed, Player A enters a number into a cell. In any other cell, Player A enters a formula that uses the cell of the number just entered. Player A presses RETURN or clicks the box. A number now replaces the formula on the spreadsheet. Player B opens her eyes and tries to discover the formula; to do this, Player B is allowed to change only the number in the first cell, where Player A entered a number. In addition, Player B can check an idea by entering it as a formula in a different cell and comparing answers.

Associated guiding questions:

- Is there a rule or relationship here?
- How are things changing?
- Does my rule work for all cases?

You may want to limit the kinds of formulas that are allowable. For instance, if you want your students to work only with formulas of the form $y = ax + b$, you should tell them that formulas can use the cell number only once and that they should use only the operations addition, subtraction, and multiplication. If you do not limit the possible formulas, students may come up with formulas that are too difficult to identify based on knowing only the outputs for a select number of inputs.

Some students may need help in developing a strategy to build the rule reflected in the spreadsheet. You might want to have a discussion with students about what strategies make the most sense.

Gum Problem

While students often have opportunities to build and use algorithms, it is also important for them to have practice understanding why specific algorithms work. This problem asks students to explain why an alternative algorithm for adding fractions works.

Gum Problem[11]

1. Jack has 2 packs of gum, a 5-pack of spearmint and a 5-pack of cinnamon. He chews 2 sticks of the spearmint and 1 stick of the cinnamon gum. He says he has chewed $2/5 + 1/5 = (2 + 1)/(5 + 5) = 3/10$ of the gum. Explain this way of adding fractions. Why does it work?

2. In Hilary's class, one-fifth of the boys are absent and two-fifths of the girls are absent. What fraction of the class is absent?

Associated guiding questions:

- How does the rule work?

- How do the numbers in the equation relate to the problem context?

- How does this expression behave like that one?

Questions can help in coming up with a solution to the first part of this problem: Is Jack right? Does the rule work? Would you have used a different algorithm? How does your algorithm compare with this algorithm? What does $2/5 + 1/5$ represent? When Jack writes down that he has chewed $2/5 + 1/5$ of the gum, he is representing something other than $3/5$. In his head, he is thinking "2/5 of the spearmint plus 1/5 of the cinnamon." The proper fractions to add are 2/10 and 1/10. Thus, in Jack's second step, he corrects himself and inserts the right denominator to come up with the answer.

Part two of this activity reveals why more than a knowledge of computational algorithms may be needed to solve fraction problems. How is this situation similar to or different from the situation with the gum in Jack's problem? The situation is similar in that the same two fractions appear. The major difference, of course, is that, in Hilary's problem, we don't know the units we are dealing with—neither the numbers of boys and girls nor the total number of students in the class.

If the number of boys in the class is the same as the number of girls, then the situation is like that in the gum problem. If x is the number of boys (and girls), then $x/5 + 2x/5 = 3x/5$ is the total number absent. Dividing this by the total number of students, $2x$, reveals that $3/10$ is the fraction of the total class absent.

Algorithm Extensions

In addition to building, using, and understanding algorithms, students can deepen their understanding of them by practicing extending algorithms to other settings. In doing this, students must abstract essential elements from the original situation and translate them into a different context.

Algorithm Extensions[12]

Given any two integers, recall an algorithm for finding their greatest common divisor. (See the appendix at the end of this chapter for one such algorithm—the Euclidean algorithm.) Now think about trinomials. What would "the greatest common divisor of two trinomials" mean? Find two trinomials, the greatest common divisor of which is a binomial. What would be an algorithm for finding the greatest common divisor of any two trinomials?

Associated guiding questions:

- How is this calculating situation like/unlike that one?
- When I do the same thing with different objects, what still holds true? What changes?

This problem can be approached with varying levels of sophistication by students at different levels. It forces students to examine the underlying structure of the integers and the polynomials, find parallels between these two systems, and link the two by relating algorithms for finding the greatest common divisor.

Students must first extend their notion of greatest common divisor to the polynomial setting. Extending the notion of "common divisor" to the polynomial setting is much easier for students than is extending the notion of "greatest" common divisor. Questions that might help include the following: How might one polynomial be "greater" than another? The greatest common divisor of two integers is the largest of the common divisors. What other properties does this number have in relation to other common divisors? How might this be extended to the polynomial setting?

For example, one could make the following definition: the polynomial $f(x)$ is greater than $g(x)$ if the leading coefficient of $f(x)$ is greater than the leading coefficient of $g(x)$. Then, for example, $4x + 1$ would be "greater" than $2x^2 + 1$. However, this definition contains features that would make it impossible to extend the notion of greatest common divisor from the integers to the polynomial setting. In the integers, a greatest common divisor is not only the largest of all the common divisors, but also the common divisor into which all other common divisors divide evenly. The definition for *greatest common divisor* in the polynomial setting should retain this quality: A polynomial that is a greatest common divisor should be a common divisor into which all other common divisors divide evenly. The definition provided above, based on leading coefficients, does not meet this requirement.

Once students have established a definition for *greatest common divisor* in the polynomial setting, they can move to extending the Euclidean algorithm to the polynomial setting.

Notes

1. From *Make It Simpler,* by Carol Meyer and Tom Sallee; copyright 1983 by Addison–Wesley Publishing Company. Reprinted by permission.
2. This version of this problem was developed by Al Cuoco and the EDC staff for EDC professional development projects.
3. This activity is based on a problem in Bowers, H. & J. Bowers. 1961. *Arithmetical Excursions,* 227. New York: Dover.
4. Excerpted from "Patterns," *Interactive Mathematics Program Year 1*, copyright 1997 by Interactive Mathematics Program. Published by Key Curriculum Press (Emeryville, CA).
5. This version of this problem was developed by Al Cuoco and the EDC staff for EDC professional development projects.
6. A similar version of this problem appears in *MathScape: Seeing and Thinking Mathematically, Patterns in Numbers and Shapes, Lesson 10.* 1998. Mountain View, CA: Creative Publications.
7. This version of this activity was developed by the EDC staff for professional development projects; it can be found in various materials, such as the *Interactive Mathematics Program.*
8. This activity is from *Connected Geometry: Cut and Rearrange.* 2000. Chicago: Everyday Learning Co. 164.
9. Excerpted from "Patterns," *Interactive Mathematics Program Year 1*, copyright 1997 by Interactive Mathematics Program. Published by Key Curriculum Press (Emeryville, CA).
10. This problem is adapted from a problem in *MathScape: Seeing and Thinking Mathematically, Getting Down to Business, Lesson 5.* 1998. Mountain View, CA: Creative Publications.
11. This problem was adapted from a set of professional development activities developed for EDC projects by Jim Hammerman and Ellen Davidson.
12. This activity is adapted from professional development materials developed for EDC projects by Al Cuoco.

13. This activity is adapted from professional development materials developed for EDC projects by Al Cuoco.

References and Further Reading

Bradley, E.H. 1997. "Is Algebra in the Cards?" *Mathematics Teaching in the Middle School* 2 (6): 398–403.

Cuoco, A. 1992. *Action to Process: Constructing Functions from Algebra Word Problems.* Newton, MA: Education Development Center.

Hammerman, J. 1995. "Teacher Inquiry Groups: Collaborative Explorations of Changing Practice." In *Inquiry and the Development of Teaching,* ed. B. Newson, 47–55. Newton, MA: Education Development Center.

Meyer, C. & T. Sallee. 1983. *Make It Simpler: A Practical Guide to Problem Solving in Mathematics.* Menlo Park, CA: Addison Wesley.

Niven, I., H.S. Zuckerman & H.L. Montgomery. 1991. *An Introduction to the Theory of Numbers.* New York: John Wiley and Sons.

Quinn, R.J. 1997. "Developing Conceptual Understanding of Relations and Functions with Attribute Blocks." *Mathematics Teaching in the Middle School* 3 (3): 186–90.

Rubenstein, R.N. 1996. "The Function Game." *Mathematics Teaching in the Middle School* 2 (2): 74–78.

Russell, S.J. et al. 1995. "Learning Mathematics While Teaching." In *Inquiry and the Development of Teaching,* ed. B. Nelson, 9–16. Newton, MA: Education Development Center.

Appendix: The Euclidean Algorithm[13]

The Euclidean algorithm is based on one of the most important calculations in arithmetic:

$$
\begin{array}{r}
14 \\
216 \overline{)3162} \\
\underline{3024}
\end{array}
$$

The process here is to start with two integers, *a* and *b*; divide the smaller into the larger, obtaining a remainder *r*; and then to repeat the process with *r* and the smaller of *a* and *b*. Keep doing this until the remainder is 0. Two facts:

1. You *will* always get to 0 eventually.

2. The last nonzero remainder is the greatest common divisor of *a* and *b*.

So, for example, the greatest common divisor of 216 and 3,162 is 6, because 6 is the last nonzero remainder in the sequence of the foregoing calculations. The reason this works is not at all obvious or straightforward; for a full discussion, see any elementary number theory book, such as *An Introduction to the Theory of Numbers*, by Niven, Zuckerman, and Montgomery.

3

Building on Number Sense and Number Theory

Background

The previous chapter noted how foreign "algebra" can look to students, and how it can seem to be a system of symbols and rules with little connection to the number and computational work done in previous grades. We argued for the value of smoothing the transition to algebra by capitalizing on students' propensities for thinking in terms of rule-based processes. To capitalize on such thinking means making the use of rules explicit in classroom debriefing of problems and helping students to think algorithmically about the actions that a particular process comprises—to think of the process as an entity that takes input and yields output.

One central message of this book is that algebraic-thinking habits of mind can develop in the classroom in many situations wherein the material being covered is not explicitly "algebraic" in appearance, but wherein a few well-placed questions can tap the material to foster algebraic thinking. For many teachers, this requires a rethinking of the content they teach, in order to root algebraic thinking more firmly in the prealgebra years.

It is the kind of rethinking exemplified by the experience of one of the teachers who participated in our projects. Valerie is a middle-grades teacher who was particularly vocal during a LUMR summer institute about her perspective that success in algebra grew out of success in arithmetic, asking several times in the first few days, "But isn't it essential that students master basic skills before they can succeed in algebra?" By "basic skills," she said she meant a fair degree of accuracy in using computational algorithms.

About a week into the institute, the teachers worked in small groups on the following activity (which we will return to in greater depth later in the chapter), which was intended to spur algebraic thinking through the use of elementary number theory.

Something Nu

Consider the operation of counting the factors of a whole number. This function is usually called "ν" (the lowercase Greek letter for "nu"). For example, the number 6 has the factors 1, 2, 3, and 6, so $\nu(6) = 4$. Here's some practice:

1. If the input to v is 5, what is the output? What if the input is 12?

2. What is $v(24)$? $v(288)$? $v(2^3 \times 3^2 \times 5^4)$?

3. Find some numbers that v takes to 6.

4. Classify all numbers n so that $v(n) = 3$. Classify all numbers n so that $v(n) = 2$.

5. What can you say about a number m if $v(m) = 12$?

6. Find two numbers n and m so that $v(nm) = v(n)v(m)$. Find two more. Compare with what other people have found.

After the small groups had done some reporting back on these questions and on some extensions, and after the full group had discussed the different ways that people had thought about the questions, Valerie raised her hand and said, "I see. Algebra can be based on number theory as much as on arithmetic!" As she explained it, she saw the potential for taking rather mundane number-sense topics, such as factors of whole numbers, and asking questions about the underlying number concepts that foreshadow algebraic concerns.

In this chapter, we advocate a shift in perspective, like Valerie's, and focus on the opportunities for fostering algebraic thinking through number-theory experiences. In particular, we focus on opportunities to help students develop the habits of mind described in Chapter 1. For example, in the Something Nu activity, there is a direct invitation to think in terms of Building Rules to Represent Functions by framing "number of factors" as a functional relation, and talking about the input and output of this function. Similarly, there is an appeal to Doing–Undoing in challenges such as, "Find some numbers that v takes to 6."

Issues of Student Understanding

If, as we believe, there is potential to mine algebraic thinking in students' efforts to understand and use the concept of *number*, then it is important to look at some issues of student understanding for the concept of number. Because our projects have featured regular discussions among teachers about student work, we have been able to track issues about student understanding that arise regularly. One issue has to do with how students can become mired when thinking in terms of *infinite sets* of numbers. Take, for example, the foregoing Something Nu questions. It could be far more challenging for a student to answer, "Classify all numbers n so that $v(n) = 3$," than it would be to answer, "What is a number that has output of 3?" The latter can be answered by trial and error, a strategy that cannot, on its own, lead to an answer for the first task, which involves an infinite set.

With regard to student understanding of number and its bearing on algebraic thinking, we have been led to wonder

- Whether some students find it difficult to think in terms of infinite sets or infinite sequences of numbers, in particular, those in which all elements share the same characteristic, say, "powers of 2."

- How important a facility with infinite number sets and/or sequences is to the development of algebraic thinking. For example, what influence might it have on the capacity to work with algebraic expressions such as $4y + 2$, in which it is implied that y takes on an infinite number of values?

The following two stories are drawn from the efforts of teachers to use student work as a lens on algebraic thinking. Using student work can hone attention to what is important in algebraic thinking, in these cases, attending to and wondering about the importance of students' facility with infinite sets and sequences.

Story 1: A Matter of Recognition or Understanding?

This first incident took place during the second year of the LUMR project, at a monthly team meeting in one of our six cities, in which teachers were analyzing student work on Sums of Consecutive Numbers. (See Chapter 2 for an explication of this activity.) To maximize student access to the activity, many of the middle-grades teachers in the group had asked their students to concentrate on answering the questions about sums of consecutive numbers from 1 to 35.

Consistent with the structure of the project, the meeting was led by two teacher–facilitators. In the full-group discussion, after small-group analyses of student work, the facilitators gleaned and listed a range of comments and questions. From across the groups there were observations that, while a few students mentioned "powers of 2" to refer to the numbers that could not be expressed as sums of consecutive numbers, many merely listed 1, 2, 4, 8, 16, and 32 without classifying them as powers of 2. Was this a lack of recognition by the students of the powers of 2 as a way of characterizing the set of numbers with which they were working? Did this imply that they, as teachers, needed to address the issue of correct use of mathematical vocabulary? Toward the end of this discussion, as time was running out, one of the teachers asked, "What were we looking for, anyway? To see whether they recognized the powers of 2?" Given that the project's focus was algebraic thinking, the teacher's question could be taken in part as asking, "What connections, if any, are there to algebraic thinking in this phenomenon we've been talking about?"

So, what *was* important here—vocabulary or something else? What, to use the teacher's words, "were we looking for, anyway?" It did seem worth wondering why so many students failed to characterize the set $\{1, 2, 4, 8, 16, 32\}$ as "powers of 2." Was it a matter of lack of recognition? Of a lack of appropriate mathematical vocabulary? Perhaps it was the way the middle-grades teachers had focused the task: Many of the students had limited their work to the numbers 1 to 35, so writing the set of six numbers sufficed, and any reference to "powers of 2" was almost irrelevant. Nonetheless, the issue of *understanding and characterizing infinite sets* was raised, and we have come to believe that it is a consideration that all teachers of prealgebra and algebra should bring to their expectations about student understanding of infinite sets.

Story 2: How Students Characterize Infinite Number Sets

At another LUMR site, teachers found similar reasons to wonder about students' characterization of infinite number sets when their students worked on the Locker problem (also discussed in Chapter 1).

As you may recall from the discussion of the activity, it turns out that the lockers that are still open after all the changes have been made have numbers that match the perfect squares $\{1, 4, 9, 16, 25, 36, \text{etc.}\}$. As revealed in the student work gathered in LUMR, many students do not recognize or characterize these as perfect squares. Some characterize the numbers, not in terms of the entire set, but recursively, in terms of how each number is related to the one before. For example, the LUMR team puzzled over the following piece of student work. Look at Figure 3–1 to see what the student does with the sequence of perfect squares (in the upper right side).

There is nothing wrong with this student's response; in fact, it brings to the surface an important feature of the perfect squares that isn't always recognized, namely, consecutive squares are separated by consecutive odd numbers 3, 5, 7, and so on. (Alternatively, as the student records it, there are successively, 2, 4, 6, etc., numbers lying between consecutive squares.) Faced with a sequence of numbers, learners can pay attention to it in several ways. They can ignore the size of the set, infinite or not, and pay attention to whether and how each element is related to its neighbors in the sequence, as this student has. Alternatively, they can ignore such "recursive" concerns and consider the set as a whole and look for characteristics

FIGURE 3–1. *Student's Characterization of Infinite Number Set*

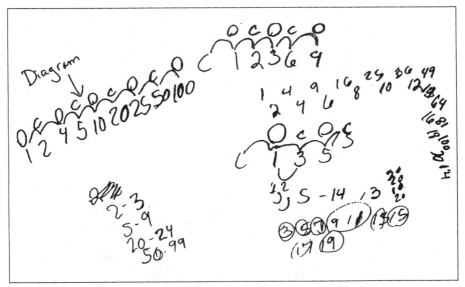

common across the entire set (e.g., powers of 2, or perfect squares). Ideally, we want students to be facile with infinite number sets in both ways, but it is important to take stock, as did the LUMR teachers, that students do not all think about infinite number sets in the same way.

Another reason to keep in mind how students think about infinite sets is the difficulty that many students have in working with algebraic expressions like $4n + 2$, in which it is implied that y can take on an infinite number of values. It is true that one likely factor in the difficulty is the association that students develop between unknowns such as n or x and statements of equality, such as $4n + 2 = 6$, in which the letter generally stands for a single number (Wagner & Parker 1993). However, it is also worth attending to the fact that thinking of the infinite set of numbers $4n + 2$, in which, say, n can stand for any integer, is not a trivial task. This is especially true for younger students, but it can affect older ones as well.

Another consideration about student understanding of number is the depth of their understanding of *divisibility*, that is, what it means for one number to be evenly divisible by another. This concept seems to be pivotal in learners' development of an abstract understanding of number and number systems, and, significantly, due to our emphasis on habits of mind, it also seems to be pivotal for acquiring the capacity to abstract from computation. There is convincing research evidence that understanding how to factor numbers is not equivalent to understanding divisibility. Asked if $5^2 3^3 7$ is divisible by 7, it is not uncommon for even college-aged students to multiply it out before they can answer (Zazkis & Campbell 1996).

The research shows that an understanding of the concept of divisibility develops in stages. For example, consider the question, "Between the numbers 26,132 and 26,152, is there a number divisible by 13?" At early stages of thinking about the concept of divisibility, learners will approach this by dividing 13 into 26,132; then into 26,133; and so on, until a number is found that is divisible by 13 (Zazkis & Campbell 1996). At later stages, the concept of divisibility will be developed well enough so that learners will be able to apply a deeper understanding of regularity in divisibility; in this case, such thinking might resemble, "Well, I know that, starting with 0, numbers divisible by 13 occur every 13 numbers. Since 26,132 and 26,152 are 20 apart from each other, there must be some number in between them that is divisible by 13." This is more advanced, in part, because of the second element.

Recommendations for Ongoing Attention to Number Work

It seems likely that some students do find infinite sets difficult, that the difficulties do impede their understanding and use of algebraic expressions, and that teachers ought to make explicit use of discussions about infinite sets when opportunities arise in working with number. Here are some suggestions for regularly capitalizing on students' number work.

Identify Curriculum Units with Number-Sense Opportunities

Many of the most recent curriculum materials for the elementary and middle school years include a variety of activities that are geared to develop number sense. In these experiences for students, there are potential foreshadowings of algebra, for example, in the recognition and representation of functional relations. For example, as the teacher Valerie pointed out in the earlier anecdote, opportunities for nurturing algebraic-thinking habits of mind arise in activities on the factoring of whole numbers that are a common feature of many curricula in the prealgebra years. They are mainly focused on developing students' understanding of the structure of the number system (evens, odds, primes, etc.) and students' skills in factoring. However, it is possible to build algebraic-thinking habits of mind while pursuing these goals.

Apply an Algebraic-Thinking Habits-of-Mind Perspective to Number Activities

It can be constructive to talk about factoring in functional terms, thus invoking the habit Building Rules to Represent Functions, as in relating a whole number (input) with the number of its factors (output). "If the input is 36, what is the output?" "What is a number that has the same output as does 36?" This opens the door for fostering another algebraic-thinking habit of mind, Doing–Undoing, asking students to reverse their thinking. "What is a number that has output of 5?"

- More advanced questions in this vein are the following: "For the function that takes any whole number as input and produces the number of its factors as output, what does its graph look like?" "What are all the numbers that have an output of 3?" The first question requires thinking about representing unfamiliar functional rules; the second requires "undoing" that involves an infinite set of numbers.

- The third algebraic-thinking habit of mind we are considering in this book is Abstracting from Computation. Work with numbers can serve to foster the development of this habit of mind, as well, when it invites learners to apply features of the number system that they see as universally true, rather than to compute each time with specific numbers. Since the concept of divisibility seems so pivotal and also relatively complex, teachers can and should ask occasional questions that push at an understanding of divisibility, such as, "Between 5241 and 5261, is there a number divisible by 13? by 17? by 8? How did you decide?"

- Long before they are expected to manipulate algebraic expressions such as $4n + 2$, middle schoolers can engage with questions that build their facility with infinite number sets, such as the following: "Think of all the thin rectangles that have one side equal to 1 unit and the other side equal to an even number of units. Will any such rectangle have a perimeter equal to 480 units? Will any have a perimeter that is a multiple of 8? Why or why not?" Though algebra as a language provides the means to be concise here (e.g., "All perimeters of such rectangles will be of the form $4n + 2$, and both 480 and any multiple of 8 are of the form $4n$."), it is possible to come up with a convincing and thorough nonsymbolic explanation (e.g., "The perimeters of these rectangles are 6, 10, 14, 18, 22, etc., and none of these numbers can be divided by 4, like 480 can. And, if they can't be divided by 4, they can't be divided by 8.").

- Algebra can confound students with its frequent use of the word *always*, as in "$x^2 - y^2$ will always be equal to $(x + y)(x - y)$, no matter what x and y are." Again, there are a host of opportunities from the prealgebra years onward, drawn from work with numbers, that can foster an appreciation of *always* in mathematics; for example, in prealgebra: "If you multiply three consecutive whole numbers, what will always be true about the product, no matter what three consecutive numbers you choose?"; or, later, in an algebra course: "The product of three consecutive integers is divisible by 6. The product of four consecutive integers is divisible by 24. Investigate a generalization of these two assertions."

- Teachers should give the word *always* a special role in classroom mathematical discourse, and question the meaning attached to it whenever students use it in numerical situations. In the same vein, teachers can occasionally ask questions that incorporate the word, such as, "Do you think that will always be true for every whole number?"

- Whenever teachers opt to limit the range of focus for students (e.g., as the LUMR teachers restricted attention in Sums of Consecutive Numbers to the integers from 1 to 35), in order to widen student access, they make sure to challenge students, once they have a set of conclusions, to try to extend their conclusions to a wider number range (e.g., to all positive integers).

- Another step teachers can take is to make conscious use of the algebraic potential in the infinite natural-number sequences that are accessible to their students. For example:

1. multiples of 3

2. multiples of 5

3. powers of 2

4. powers of 3

5. perfect squares

6. perfect cubes

7. primes

By asking a variety of questions about the internal structures and interrelationships of these sequences, it is possible to involve all three algebraic-thinking habits of mind. For example, "For any two pairs of sequences (e.g., A and F), are there numbers that are in both?" will engage students in Doing–Undoing, because they will be obliged (if the two sequences are A and F) to wonder under what conditions a multiple of 3 (i.e., a number of the form $3m$) can also be a perfect cube (i.e., a number of the form n^3).

Crossfield (1997) demonstrates from his own teaching experience the many algebraic questions that can be asked about the relationships within and between these different sequences. We revisit his suggested activities in the next section, which highlights example activities teachers can try.

Example Activities

The following activities can be used to foster algebraic thinking in number contexts and to provide students with experiences with infinite sets. Occasionally, in italics, we list some of the relevant algebraic-thinking guiding questions that were discussed in Chapter 1.

Stretching Problem

The Stretching problem provides opportunities to engage with number factors, and it can be used to lay the groundwork for other challenges involving factoring, such as the Locker problem and two that are discussed in this section, Something Nu and Lucky Lockers.

Stretching Problem[1]

At the Bubble Gum Factory, lengths of gum are stretched to larger lengths by putting them through stretching machines. There are 100 stretching machines, numbered 1 through 100. Machine 1 does nothing to a piece of gum; machine 2 stretches pieces of gum to twice their original length; machine 3 triples the length of gum, and so forth. So, machine 23, for example, will stretch a piece of gum to 23 times its original length.

An order has just come in for a piece of bubble gum 26 inches in length. The factory has pieces of gum that are only 1 inch in length, and machine number 26 is broken. Is there any way to create a piece of bubble gum 26 inches in length by using other machines? Some of the machines in the factory are unnecessary because combinations of other machines could be used instead. Figure out which machines are actually unnecessary.

1. What machines would be necessary to get the following lengths: 15? 28? 36? 65? 84?

2. For each of the lengths in question 1, what other machines could have been used that were unnecessary?

3. Which lengths between 1 and 100 would come out if the bubble gum went through five machines and all five machines were necessary ones?

4 Which lengths between 1 and 100 require the greatest number of necessary machines? How did you figure out your answer?

The machines whose numbers are primes are the necessary machines; all others are unnecessary. Lengths of 32, 48, 72, and 80 inches require exactly five necessary machines. For example, a length of 32 inches requires machine number 2 to be used five times in succession. The greatest number of necessary machines needed to produce a length between 1 and 100 inches is six; six machines are required to produce gum that is 64 inches long and 96 inches long. Once questions have been answered for the case of 1 to 100, the problem can be extended, say, to 200. Now, the algebraic-thinking habits of mind and associated guiding questions grow more relevant: *What changes and what stays the same? Is there new information here that lets me predict what is going to happen?* Questions can flow back and forth between doing and undoing: How many machines are necessary for a 160-inch length? Which lengths between 100 and 200 inches require six necessary machines? Seven?

Something Nu

This is the activity cited in the first section of this chapter, which helped Valerie shift her perspective about the roots of prealgebra. It, too, is concerned with factorization of whole numbers.

Something Nu

Consider the operation of counting the factors of a whole number. This function is usually called "v" (the lowercase Greek letter for "nu"). For example, the number 6 has the factors 1, 2, 3, and 6, so $v(6) = 4$. Here's some practice:

1. If the input to v is 5, what is the output? What if the input is 12?

2. What is $v(24)$? $v(288)$? $v(2^3 \times 3^2 \times 5^4)$?

3. Find some numbers that v takes to 6.

4. Classify all numbers n so that $v(n) = 3$. Classify all numbers n so that $v(n) = 2$.

5. What can you say about a number m if $v(m) = 12$?

6. Find two numbers n and m so that $v(nm) = v(n)v(m)$. Find two more. Compare with what other people have found.

This activity introduces an input–output perspective into what might otherwise be experienced as yet another mathematical procedure, this one a procedure for counting factors. Furthermore, giving the output, like 2, and asking for the input fosters Doing–Undoing, which is another habit of mind key to effective algebraic thinking. Lastly, framing set-classification questions such as these ("Classify all n . . ." or "What are all the numbers . . .?") is a way to engage in, and to engage students in, thinking about infinite sets of numbers.

Because the factors of 5 are 1 and 5, $V(5) = 2$. Because the factors of 12 are 1, 2, 3, 4, 6, and 12, $V(12) = 6$. Some students think that because 24 is 2 times 12, $V(24)$ will be twice as large as $V(12)$. Is it? Why doesn't this student notion work? In the analysis of the Locker problem in Chapter 1, we introduced the function V and introduced a formula for computing the number of factors for any whole number, based on its prime factorization. Using this formula for $2^3 \times 3^2 \times 5^4 = 45,000$, we get $V(2^3 \times 3^2 \times 5^4) = (3 + 1)(2 + 1)(4 + 1) = 60$.

Invoking the formula again, we can say that if V takes a number n to $3 = 2 + 1$, n must be of the form p^2, for some prime number p. Similarly, if $V(m) = 12$, since $12 = (2 + 1)(1 + 1)(1 + 1)$ and since 12 also equals $(2 + 1)(3 + 1)$, then m could be of the form p^2qr for any different primes p, q, r; or m could be of the form p^2q^3 for any different primes p and q. Is there another possibility?

Lastly, another analysis of the formula will lead to the conclusion that for $V(nm)$ to equal $V(n)V(m)$, n and m must have no common factors except 1; that is, they are relatively prime.

Differences of Squares

Here is another question, set in a number context, that elicits all three habits of mind on which we are concentrating in this book: Building Rules to Represent Functions, Abstracting from Computation, and Doing–Undoing. Additionally, the Differences of Squares problem can be used to push on students' conception of *always* and gives students practice working with and characterizing infinite sets of numbers.

Differences of Squares

Which numbers can be expressed as the difference of two perfect squares?

Create a list of the first seven perfect squares. What patterns do you see in the differences among these consecutive squares? The difference between 1 and 4 is 3; the difference between 4 and 9 is 5; the difference between 9 and 16 is 7. We can generalize this pattern: The difference between n^2 and $(n + 1)^2$ is $2n + 1$. Hence, all odd numbers can be represented as a difference of two squares. (Recall what the student, whose work on the Locker problem is illustrated in Figure 3–1, did with the sequence of perfect squares.)

What about even numbers? (*When I do the same thing with different numbers, what still holds true? What changes?*) There are several ways to approach this part of the problem. First, we could use what we know from the odd case to come up with an approach to this part of the problem. Because the sequence of differences of consecutive squares is the set of odd numbers, we know that the difference between any two squares must be represented as a sum of consecutive odd numbers. For example:

$6^2 - 2^2 = (6^2 - 5^2) + (5^2 - 4^2) + (4^2 - 3^2) + (3^2 - 2^2)$ (*How can I write the expression in terms of things I care about?*), which in turn is equal to $11 + 9 + 7 + 5$, the sum of four consecutive odd numbers. Once we realize this, our question changes. Rather than "What even numbers can be expressed as the differences of perfect squares," we can ask, "How can we characterize the numbers that are sums of consecutive odd numbers?"

Alternatively, we might notice that the difference between n^2 and $(n + 2)^2$ is $4n + 4$. So, given a multiple of 4—all of which are of the form $4n + 4 = 4(n + 1)$, for some n—we can find two squares whose difference is that number. This then leaves us with the case of the even numbers that are not multiples of 4. After trying unsuccessfully to find such a number that is the difference between two squares, you might begin to doubt that these numbers exist. It seems impossible to express even numbers that are not divisible by 4 as the difference between two squares. Why might this be?

When you do this activity with students, regardless of strategies they use to arrive at a solution, in the end they should conclude that all numbers can be expressed as the difference between two squares, *except* for even numbers that are not multiples of 4. Younger students, in particular, may not be able to prove the "all" in the statements; they may only conjecture on the basis of a set of examples they develop. Even so, it is valuable for them to become aware that not all even numbers are alike: Some can be expressed as the difference between two perfect squares and some cannot. Such insights are representative of Abstracting from Computation and are part of the fiber of algebraic thinking.

Clocking

There are many good modular arithmetic problems that are set in a number context and emphasize algebraic habits of mind. The Clocking problem, while difficult, can be used at many grade levels to push students to build algorithmic rules about number relationships. It involves investigating the relationship between a pair of numbers and a single number, leading to the fact that the single number is the greatest common divisor (GCD) of the pair of numbers.

Clocking

Here is a pair of wheels from an old clock; the wheel on the left has 4 pegs, and the wheel on the right has 12 notches. Imagine them turning. Outline with a black crayon all the notches on the big wheel on the right that are touched by the black peg on the small wheel on the left. How many notches are touched by the black peg?

How many notches are touched by a single peg in a system that has

1. 3 pegs, 9 notches?
2. 8 pegs, 9 notches?
3. 4 pegs, 10 notches?
4. 9 pegs, 12 notches?
5. 6 pegs, 9 notches?
6. 12 pegs, 5 notches?

Can you think of a rule to tell you when the black peg will touch all the notches and when it won't? Why does your rule work? If the black peg does not touch all of the notches, how many will it touch?

The number of notches touched by a single peg is equal to the number that results when the GCD of the number of notches and the number of pegs is divided into the number of notches. So, in the pictured case, 4 is the GCD of 4 and 12, and the black peg touches 3 notches. For 8 pegs, 9 notches, the GCD is 1, so each peg touches all 9 notches.

Why does this process work the way it does? To start thinking about why this works, you might first explore numbers that are relatively prime—numbers whose GCD is 1. Why would a peg in a wheel system with relatively prime numbers of pegs and notches touch every notch? For younger students, a convincing argument about the role of the concept "relatively prime" is probably out of reach, but they can recognize that it plays a role; for older students, however, it is worth their while to spend time trying to reach an understanding of the process and crafting an argument on why it works.

Mathematically, the clockwheels suggest modular arithmetic systems, and, therefore, algebraic thinking along the lines of Abstracting from Computation. (*How is this calculating situation like/unlike that one?*) For example, saying that the equation $8x = 1$ has a solution in the system of integers modulo 9 is equivalent to saying that with 8 pegs, 9 notches, all the notches are touched by the black peg.

Threaded Pins

In essence, this problem is identical to that of Clocking; the context is the only difference. In Chapters 4 and 5, we discuss generalizing as an important aspect of algebraic thinking. One way in which generalizing can be fostered is in looking for the same mathematical structure in different contexts. The Threaded Pins problem could be used in conjunction with the Clocking problem to talk about this kind of generalizing and to help students make connections across problems.

Threaded Pins[2]

A number of pins are placed evenly around a circle. A thread is tied to one pin, and then looped tightly around a second pin. The thread is then looped tightly round a third pin so that the clockwise gap between the first and second pins is the same as the clockwise gap between the second and third pins, as illustrated in the example.

3 pins, gap of 1   5 pins, gap of 2   6 pins, gap of 3

The process is continued, always preserving the same clockwise gap until the first pin is reached. If some pin has not yet been used, the process starts again with a new thread.

Five pins with a gap of two use just one thread, while six pins with a gap of three use three threads. How many pieces of thread will be needed in general?

The number of pieces of thread is equal to the GCD of the number of pins and the gap. You can use this problem in conjunction with the Clocking problem and ask students to compare and contrast the two. To work on and discuss *both* may help students to better understand and describe the underlying process.

Reversals

This problem involves abstracting essential aspects from a series of calculations.

Reversals[3]

Take a three-digit number, reverse its digits, and subtract the smaller from the larger. Reverse the digits of the result and add. Thus,

> 123 becomes 321, and 321 − 123 = 198
> 198 becomes 891, and 198 + 891 = 1089

Try this process for several numbers. What happens? Why?

If the first and third digits are the same, the process results in a 0. If, however, the first and third digits are different, then the process always results in the number 1089. To understand why, look at the underlying process and determine what patterns hold only for the specific example in the statement of the problem and what patterns are more general. If you do this in the classroom, whether students approach the problem using symbolic notation or not, they should find that after the first step in the process (the subtraction step), they get a number, the middle digit of which is 9 and the first and third digits of which add up to 9. Adding this number to its "reversal" results in the number 1089.

Symbolically, it looks like this: Suppose the original number is $100a + 10b + c$, and $a > c$. Then, after reversing to get $100c + 10b + a$, the difference is $[100a + 10b + c] - [100c + 10b + a] = 100(a - c - 1) + 90 + (10 + c - a)$. Reversing this gives $100(10 + c - a) + 90 + (a - c - 1)$. Adding gives $100(a - c - 1) + 90 + (10 + c - a) + 100(10 + c - a) + 90 + (a - c - 1)$. This is equal to $100a - 100c - 100 + 90 + 10 + c - a + 1000 + 100c - 100a + 90 + a - c - 1$. All the c-terms and a-terms cancel out, and what is left is $-100 + 90 + 10 + 1000 + 90 - 1$, which equals 1089.

Dog Days

This problem could be given to prealgebra students to familiarize them with infinite sets. While the problem can be solved with symbolic notation, it can also be done without formal symbolic notation.

Dog Days

In general, dogs do not live as long as humans. People often estimate that humans live about seven times as long as dogs. This means that you can estimate that for every "human year," a dog goes through 7 "dog years."

Liza got a dog just before last New Year's Day. On New Year's Day, Liza and her family celebrated the dog's first birthday, in dog years. How old, in dog years, will the dog be next New Year's Day? Will the dog ever turn 51 in dog years on New Year's Day? Given an age, how can you tell whether Liza's dog will celebrate that birthday on New Year's Day?

The dog will celebrate birthdays on New Year's Day for ages of the form $7n + 1$ for all natural numbers n. *How can I describe the steps without using specific inputs?* What is important about this problem is that it gives students practice working with and characterizing infinite sets (assuming the unreasonable condition that the dog will live forever), and, when it asks whether numbers such as 51 fit, it also hones their Doing–Undoing thinking: *What process reverses the one I used?*

Olympics

As was the case with the previous problem, Dog Days, this problem gives students more practice working with infinite sets in a real-world context.

Olympics

The Winter Olympics are held every 4 years in January. The last Winter Olympics were held in Nagano, Japan, in January of 1998. When will the Winter Olympics happen next? Will the Winter Olympics be held in 2040? 2058? How can you tell whether the Winter Olympics will be held in any given year?

The Winter Olympics will be held in years of the form $4n + 2$ for natural numbers n. Students who do not use symbolic notation might describe these numbers as "even numbers not divisible by 4, " "every other even number starting with 1998," and so on. Like the Dog Days problem, this problem builds facility with infinite sets and with Doing–Undoing.

Number Fun

This activity provides students with experiences dealing with infinite sets; in particular, students have many opportunities to examine characterizing features of infinite sets and use these features to solve problems. Crossfield (1997), the originator of these activities, spends a few minutes each day examining questions of this nature, thus giving his students ongoing exposure to work with infinite sets while also developing number and operation sense.

Number Fun[4]

Consider the following sets of numbers:

> Pink Numbers: 2, 3, 5, 7, 11, 13, 17, 19, 23, 29, 31, 37, . . .
> Blue Numbers: 2, 4, 8, 16, 32, 64, 128, 256, 512, 1024, 2048, 4096, . . .
> Green Numbers: 1, 8, 27, 64, 125, 216, 343, 512, 729, 1000, 1331, . . .
> Red Numbers: 1, 4, 9, 16, 25, 36, 49, 64, 81, 100, 121, 144, 169, . . .

1. What is the next number in each sequence?

2. Can you find two numbers of the same color, the difference or sum of which is a pink number?

3. Can you find a number, the double (or twice that number) of which is the same color?

4. 64 is both red and green. What other numbers are both red and green? 512 is both green and blue. What other numbers are both green and blue?

The pink numbers are the primes; the blue numbers are powers of 2; the green numbers are cubes; and the red numbers are squares. To come up with an answer, the remaining questions require students to use what they know about what characterizes each set. The second question, in particular, draws on Abstracting from Computation, especially when students realize how much they can generalize from their examples. (*When I do the same things with different numbers, what still holds true? What changes?*) The fourth question draws on Doing–Undoing: *Can I decom-*

pose this number into helpful components? For example, the number $(64)^3 = 262{,}144$ is green because it is a cube, but it can be decomposed further into $(2^6)^3 = 2^{18}$ and so is a blue number as well.

Lucky Lockers

This problem is a more difficult follow-up to the Locker problem. The first locker problem called into play thinking algorithmically about primes and factors, in particular, about the relationship between a whole number and the number of factors it has. Though quite a bit can be done in the problem without knowing anything about the nu (ν) function, we introduced it in our analysis of the first locker problem to show the full connection between the problem and elementary number theory. Lucky Lockers pays attention to a different, but related, aspect of the factoring process.

Lucky Lockers

The eccentric principal of the school with 200 lockers has won the lottery! Now she wants to give away some of her money, but in a rather strange way. She has asked the students who opened and closed the lockers to repeat the process, but with one big difference. This time, the first student will go to each locker and place \$1 in it. The next student will go to every other locker (starting with #2) and place \$2 in it. Then another student follows, putting \$3 in every third locker. As in the Locker problem in Chapter 1, the process continues until it's impossible to put money in any locker.

1. How is this like the Locker problem in Chapter 1? How is it different?

2. How can you model this new situation?

3. What (new) questions come to mind? What conjectures or answers do you have?

Like the first locker problem, Lucky Lockers requires that students pay attention to the factors of the number on the locker. Instead of asking about the number of factors, this problem asks about the sum of the factors. So, the implicit function (ν) in the first locker problem takes a number to its number of factors; the function in Lucky Lockers (called the σ, or sigma, function) takes a number to the sum of its factors. Students in middle and high school can explore both of these functions in varying degrees of depth. In Chapter 1, we provided a formula for ν; a similar but more complex formula exists for σ. For students and teachers who are curious about the closed form of these functions, see any elementary number theory book, such as *An Introduction to the Theory of Numbers,* by Niven, Zuckerman, and Montgomery (1991, 188–91).

Short of learning about and using the formula for σ, students can explore what σ looks like for powers of small numbers, such as 2, 3, and 5, and look for patterns:

For any whole number n, $\sigma(2^n) = 1 + 2 + 4 + \ldots + 2^n$, and that is equal to $2^{n+1} - 1$. Similarly, $\sigma(3^n) = 1 + 3 + 9 + \ldots + 3^n$, and that is equal to $(3^{n+1} - 1)/2$. Going further, it turns out that $\sigma(5^n) = 1 + 5 + 25 + \ldots + 5^n$, and that is equal to $(5^{n+1} - 1)/4$. (*What are my operation shortcuts for going from here to there?*) All of these are related to the algebraic polynomial identity $1 + x + x^2 + \ldots + x^n = (x^{n+1} - 1)/(x - 1)$. However, well before students are exposed to this identity in algebra, being aware of a number identity such as $1 + 2 + 4 + \ldots + 2^n = 2^{n+1} - 1$ is helpful, in particular in developing the threads of Abstracting from Computation.

Notes

1. Excerpted from *MathScape: Seeing and Thinking Mathematically, Making Mathematical Arguments*, copyright 1998 by Creative Publications.
2. From *Thinking Mathematically*, by John Mason; copyright 1982 by Addison-Wesley Publishing Company. Reprinted by permission.
3. From *Thinking Mathematically*, by John Mason; copyright 1982 by Addison-Wesley Publishing Company. Reprinted by permission.
4. Excerpted from "(Naturally) Numbers Are Fun" by D. Crossfield, *Mathematics Teacher*, 1997, Vol. 90, No. 2.

References and Further Reading

Crossfield, D. 1997. "(Naturally) Numbers Are Fun." *Mathematics Teacher* 90: 92–95.

Johnson, I.D. 1998. "Paving the Way to Algebraic Thought Using Residue Designs." *Mathematics Teacher* 91: 326–32.

Kieran, C. & L. Chalouh. 1993. "Prealgebra: The Transition from Arithmetic to Algebra." In *Research Ideas for the Classroom: Middle Grades Mathematics*, ed. D.T. Owens, 179–98. New York: Macmillan.

Niven, I., H.S. Zuckerman & H.L. Montgomery. 1991. *An Introduction to the Theory of Numbers*. New York: John Wiley and Sons.

Stacey, K. & M. MacGregor. 1997. "Building Foundations for Algebra." *Mathematics Teaching in the Middle School* 2: 252–60.

Wagner, S. & S. Parker. 1993. "Advancing Algebra." In *Research Ideas for the Classroom: High School Mathematics*, ed. P. Wilson, 119–39. New York: Macmillan.

Zazkis, R. & S. Campbell. 1996. "Divisibility and Multiplicative Structure of Natural Numbers: Preservice Teachers' Understanding." *Journal for Research in Mathematics Education* 27: 540–63.

4

Expressing Generalizations About Structure

Importance of Generalizing

Generalizing is one of the most fundamental and important mathematical thinking processes. It is the process that allows us to look beyond the particularities of a mathematical situation and make conclusions such as, "That's a case of . . ." or "This will always hold true, as long as . . ." Students' success in learning this process, along with their success in learning the process of making convincing mathematical arguments, will strongly influence how far they go and how well they succeed in mathematics through high school and beyond.

Algebra is often referred to as "generalized arithmetic," meaning in part that letters are used to denote expressions or statements that apply to any number; for example, "Not only is $4 + 7$ equal to $7 + 4$, but $x + y$ is equal to $y + x$ for any numbers x and y." To see algebra only in this guise, however, is to misrepresent the role of generalization in algebraic thinking. For example, in Chapter 3, we argued that some aspects of algebraic thinking generalize number theory, not the structure and rules of arithmetic.

To identify algebra as generalized arithmetic can be misleading, as well—especially if it oversimplifies the challenge and induces the strategy of merely telling students they need only work by analogy; that is, what they have done with particular numbers, they now will do with letters. Wheeler (1996) calls one of the two Big Ideas related to algebra, "the idea that a general number/variable/as yet unknown number can be symbolized and operated upon as if it was a number" (322). The idea is big not only because of its power and usefulness, but also because of the cognitive demands it places on learners as they are developing the capacity to generalize. In this light, it isn't sufficient merely to *tell* students what general numbers or variables are. Also needed are frequent opportunities for students to develop habits of thinking related to generalization. This chapter explores the teacher's role in offering such opportunities.

Our projects have focused on the development of habits of mind relevant to algebra, and so have had us considering two kinds of generalization: (1) generalization about functions and relations and (2) generalization about structure and the way operations work (Figure 4–1).

Figure 4–1. *Generalizations About Functions and Relations and Operations and Structure*

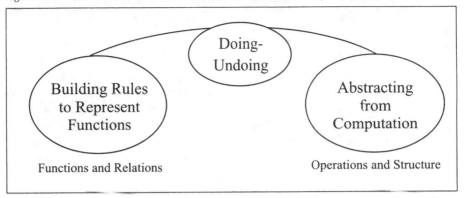

A habits-of-mind approach and our focus on the span of grades 6 through 10 give us a developmental perspective on how generalizations build on students' deep familiarity with calculation and on their prealgebra understanding and facility with functional relations.

Generalizing about functional relations is the subject of Chapter 5. Chapter 4 focuses on the kind of generalized thinking some call "operation sense" or "reasoning about operations," those insights about the way computational operations work that make possible decisions that are independent of particular numbers chosen (see, e.g., Ruopp et al. 1997). In essence, this is "calculating without calculating," taking shortcuts that are distinguished by their underlying recognition: "The calculation will produce results that are consistent, no matter what numbers I use." For example, think about the following question, and try to do it without calculating numerical answers:

"Which is greater, 4% of nine thousand dollars or 9% of four thousand dollars?"

The answer—that they are the same amount—is a realization that is quickly evident to anyone who understands commutativity for the operation of multiplication. With this understanding, it isn't necessary to pay attention to the particular numbers 4 and 9 in the problem, beyond knowing that the same pair of numbers appears in reverse order. Guiding such thinking are questions such as these: How can I predict what's going to happen without doing all the work? Where are my operation shortcut options for getting from here to there?

In other circumstances, there are other questions, also drawn from the list of guiding questions in Chapter 1, that might guide this kind of generalization; for example:

• How does this expression behave like that one?

• How is the calculating situation like/unlike that one?

• When I do the same thing with different numbers, what still holds true? What changes?

In characterizing how generalizing capacities develop in the learner, we take advantage of the fact that our projects often produce student work on the same activity administered by teachers from grades 6 through 10, and so we get a range of approaches and conclusions about what works and in how many cases. We try to understand key aspects that seem to separate the less powerful responses from the more powerful, and to determine how and to what extent instruction can address each aspect for the students producing the less powerful responses.

One also can think of how a thread of algebraic generalization grows across different content topics. For example, the use by middle-grades students of various *calculating shortcuts* based on knowing what will work in computations without reference to particular numbers, leads to the process in high school of looking for *relationships between and among systems of equations.* This thread, in turn, extends beyond high school mathematics to the process in linear algebra of *reasoning by linearity.* The next section traces this thread.

A Thread of Algebraic Generalization

Middle-Grades Mathematics

The particular thread we want to demonstrate appears in middle grades, as students build on their familiarity with operations to engage with linear combinations.[1] For example, they might start by looking at the comparative costs of combinations of shirts and socks, where shirts are 12 dollars and socks are 5 dollars:

15					
10	22				
5	17	29	41		
0	12	24	36	48	

Later, under the assumption that the following grids represent similar combination charts (not necessarily with 5 and 12 as the increments), students might be asked to find the missing numbers in

?				
	18			
0	5			

37			
27			
0		?	

			?	
	35			
		55		
0				

Such activities encourage the development of equation-solving strategies and facility with linear combinations. They also open the door for students, through the use of calculating shortcuts, to push their capacity to generalize further, as the following brief story from one of our teacher projects demonstrates.[2]

A group of middle-grades teachers worked on activities like the foregoing, and then shared solutions. On the last one, especially, the approaches varied:

1. One of the teachers showed how he set up a pair of equations to solve and find the desired number: "x is the horizontal increment and y is the vertical increment, which gives the two equations:

    $x + 2y = 35$
    $3x + y = 55$

    Then I solved these simultaneous equations, by multiplying through the second equation by 2, then subtracting the two equations to find that $x = 15$. Substituting that in the first equation gives $y = 10$. So, the question mark is really $55 + 15 + 20 = 90$."

2. Saying that she did it "the way middle-grades students would," another teacher showed how she used systematic guess-and-check processes to get the desired number: "Because 0, 35, and 55 are all multiples of 5, I figured both increments would be multiples of 5, also. So, I tried various combinations of 5, 10, 15, 20, and 25, until I settled on 10 and 15. Then I added combinations to get 90."

3. A third teacher said, "I did it a different way." Pointing to the 0, then to the 35, he said, "Over one, up two." Then pointing to the 55, then the ?, he said, "Over one, up two, so this must be 55 + 35, or 90."

All three teachers were generalizing in different ways in solving. The first seemed to be focused on "this is a case of two equations in two unknowns"—a general situation with which he was familiar—and called into play his algebraic experience. *How is this calculating situation like/unlike that one?*

The second paid attention to the numbers involved, and seemed to be generalizing on her knowledge of numbers—in particular, multiples of 5. The third teacher seemed to be attending to the underlying structure and how operations work. His solution was a case of "calculating without calculating"; that is, his "over one, up two" strategy could work no matter what numbers were given to him. *How can I predict what's going to happen without doing all the work?*

These are examples of adult thinking, but middle-grades students are certainly capable of the second and third ways of approaching the problem, if not the first. In particular, there are students who will do the kind of "calculating without calculating" that is represented in the third example, a kind of thinking that is part of a longer thread extending into high school work with systems of equations.

High School Algebra

The extension of the thread into high school touches on the algebraic challenge of comparing systems of equations. Burrill (1997) suggests the following as one of several examples she believes can encourage deep thinking about mathematics (94), and which we believe can help make calculating without calculating more habitual for students:

Consider the following systems of equations. What do they have in common and why?

$x + 2y = 3$ and $4x + 5y = 6$
$2x + 3y = 4$ and $5x + 6y = 7$
$8x + 9y = 10$ and $11x + 12y = 13$
$3x + 5y = 7$ and $9x + 11y = 13$

One approach—likely the one used by many who have taken algebra courses—is to solve each of the pairs and to answer the question by saying, "Each system has the solution pair $x = -1$, $y = 2$." However, a solution is not the only thing that the systems have in common. Thinking of each system as an entity (perhaps represented as a matrix), one can see that each is a linear combination of the other systems. For example, the fourth system is the sum of the first two; the third is seven times the second minus six times the first; and so on. It turns out that this feature among the systems—each a combination of the others—is a general condition that implies that they have the same solution. Therefore, what is gained is more generality than just solving the systems and comparing. In particular, there are concerted efforts to attend to guiding questions such as the following: How can I predict what's going to happen without doing all the calculation? What are my operation shortcuts? How does this expression behave like that one?

This thread of generalization continues beyond high school mathematics into linear algebra, where this thinking extends to what some call "reasoning by linearity." In Appendix A, we offer an example in a discussion of Cramer's Rule.

Development of the Capacity to Generalize

Occasionally, when we discuss generalization with our cross-grades groupings of teachers, a teacher will ask, "It will look different at different grades, won't it?" If the questioner is a middle-grades teacher, the question often has two meanings. First, there is genuine curiosity about how a thread of generalization looks at different points of its development. Second, the question also is intended to check expectations, to make sure we aren't expecting sixth-graders' work on an activity to look like ninth-graders' work on the same activity.

Both meanings of the question are important, because they point to two important aspects of building students' capacities to generalize: *understanding how generalization develops* and *having appropriate expectations.* To help with the understanding, we reviewed some of the student work gathered in the LUMR project for the activity Sums of Consecutive Numbers (see Chapter 2). As we made rough groupings according to level of generalization, there seemed to be three different levels. We put together composite statements which students at each level might make in response to the question: "What patterns do you see in the sums of consecutive numbers you found?"

Student A: "All numbers that are sums of three consecutive numbers can be divided by 3." (Note: "All" may be limited to the numbers 1 to 35, if the student hasn't generated any examples beyond 35.)

Student B: "All numbers that are sums of three consecutive numbers are divisible by 3: If you call the middle of the three numbers n, then the other two are $n - 1$ and $n + 1$. The sum is going to be $(n - 1) + n + (n + 1)$, which is $3n$. That's divisible by 3." (The student may or may not make a similar statement for another number, such as saying something like "The same works for the number 5.")

Student C: "To see whether a number N is a consecutive sum of m numbers, check to see if m divides N. If it does and m is odd, you know N can be written as m consecutive numbers. You divide N by m . . . call the result k. Then the consecutive numbers are: . . . , $k - 1, k, k + 1, . . .$

Example: $42 \div 7$ is 6. So, 3, 4, 5, 6, 7, 8, 9 are seven consecutive numbers that add to get 42."

Student C, especially, seems to exemplify a direction of wonder that might be associated with the habit of mind Abstracting from Computation. The student is guided by questions such as, How can I predict what's going to happen without doing all the calculation? When I do the same things with different numbers, what still holds true? What changes? In particular, this seems to be expressed in the successive subtractions of 1 to balance out successive additions of 1. Meanwhile, it is possible to imagine that behind Student B's response is also the question, "When I do the same things with different numbers, what still holds true?"—though at a different level of generality.

Student A seems to exemplify what Friedlander and Hershkowitz call a *working generalization*, "an intuitive sense of a general pattern, which can be elicited by certain tasks" (Friedlander & Hershkowitz 1997, 443). On the other hand, a case could be made that Student C has made an *explicit generalization* and has justified it with the argument about balancing the additions with the subtractions. As for Student B, things are not so clear. What is keeping him or her from making the kind of explicit generalization made by Student C? Is it the way the task was constructed and worded—a lack of clarity, perhaps? Is it that Student B has not been exposed to standards for making explicit generalizations and justifications? Or, is there something inherent in the way Student B is currently thinking about numbers and operations on numbers that places a real obstacle to thinking like Student C?

All of these are questions to guide teachers' understanding of their students' capacities to generalize. The next section looks at some aspects of setting expectations and supporting students in regard to algebraic generalizations.

Recommendations for Ongoing Attention to Generalizing About Operations and Calculations

A core principle of the Linked Learning Project is that teachers can foster algebraic thinking through their classroom questions, even when the lesson they are teaching doesn't look particularly "algebraic." This is especially true regarding the kind of calculation-based generalization that is the topic of this chapter. Problems that can be solved with direct calculation often can be enriched by asking students to pay attention to the advantages of looking for calculating shortcuts, based on operation sense.

Here is an example from a middle-grades classroom. The lesson revolved around a problem called "Skyscraper Windows":

Skyscraper Windows

You manage the Milwaukee Skyscraper building. This building is 12 stories high and is covered entirely by windows on all four sides. Once a year, all the windows are washed. The cost for washing the windows is $2.00 for each first-floor window, $2.50 for each second-floor window, $3.00 for each third-floor window, and so on. You have budgeted $2500 for window washing for the next year. Will this be enough to wash all of the windows? By how much are you off (+ or –)? (A picture of the building shows that it has 38 windows per floor.)[3]

This lesson was documented for the project by classroom observers, so we were able to see how the teacher worked to elicit algebraic thinking. As stated, the activity is a fairly straightforward arithmetic problem. In fact, many students found the answer by multiplying 38 times $2.00, adding that to the product of 38 and $2.50, and so on until the twelfth floor was reached. They then compared the total to $2500.

Toward the end of the class, as recorded by the observer, the teacher said a couple of things that opened the door for algebraic thinking (i.e., invited the students to make some generalizations):

"Suppose the building is 30 stories tall and we have $40,000. Is that enough money?"

"Once you have made a chart, look for an easier way. Pay attention to how the numbers group. How might the groupings suggest an easier way."

Of course the first question could still be answered by arithmetic, though the task starts to get cumbersome with 30 stories, but the teacher pushes the algebraic point by asking the students to look for a shortcut based on "how the numbers group" together. This draws the students' attention to what is nice and ordered about the sequence $1.50, $2.00, $2.50, and so on, and how it lends itself to calculating shortcuts. There are different ways to think of how "the numbers group." For example, five of them—$1.50, $2.00, $2.50, $3.00, $3.50—have the same sum as 5 times the middle one, $2.50. So, it isn't necessary to add them all; I just multiply 5 by $2.50. This is a short step from the more general, algebraic realization that the sum of x, $x + 50$, $x + 100$, $x + 150$, $x + 200$ is the same as 5 times $(x + 100)$.

The teacher's two questions could be generalized to many lessons in which students are asked to incorporate a sequence of numbers into a computation. The first question motivates the use of calculating shortcuts by extending the original question to a sequence long enough to make it cumbersome to do a direct computation. (When I do the same thing with different numbers, what still holds true?) The second question draws the students' attention to aspects in the sequence that might make shortcuts possible. (What are my operation shortcut options for getting from here to there?) A central belief in the Linked Learning project is that, if students are provided a fairly steady diet of opportunities—prompted by teacher questioning—to try different cases and to look for such calculating shortcuts, they are primed to develop algebraic habits of mind, even before they take algebra.

The teacher's two questions also suggest an answer to the question about appropriate expectations. Whatever defines a question that a teacher finds profitable to ask over and over again to foster algebraic thinking, should also define expectations for student efforts at generalization—in this case:

- the expectation that students will look beyond easy cases to wonder how a problem is solved in more difficult cases (e.g., with much larger numbers)

- the expectation that students will be on the lookout for calculating shortcuts in solving problems

What are other ways to create such opportunities for building the capacities to generalize? Friedlander and Hershkowitz (1997) make the distinction between "working generalization" and "explicit generalization." By *working generalization*, they mean an intuitive sense of a general pattern, which can be elicited by certain tasks and applied to solve them efficiently. A working generalization permits learners to produce additional examples within a problem, to produce and solve examples with large numbers, and to solve "reversal" tasks, which we call "undoing" tasks. They illustrate with the following example:

Launch: Solve and compare results:

$4 \times 4 =$	$8 \times 8 =$	$12 \times 12 =$
$5 \times 3 =$	$9 \times 7 =$	$13 \times 11 =$

Toward a Working Generalization: Find some other pairs of similar exercises and solve them.

Given: $256 \times 256 = 65,536$ Find: $257 \times 255 =$

Find the missing pair of numbers: $16 \times 16 = 256$, $\_ \times \_ = 255$

Toward an Explicit Generalization: Try to find a general rule that applies to all of the foregoing exercises.

Toward a Justification: Is the rule you found always true? How would you prove or convince others that your claim is true?

One further resource for thinking about supporting students in generalization, along the lines of our three habits of mind, is the guide we provided teachers in the Linked Learning in Mathematics Project (LLMP) for their final student interview. The teachers interviewed three of their students at three points during the year, as they worked on mathematics investigations. For the last interview, when the students were to work on Sums of Consecutive Numbers, we provided examples of what the different kinds of generalization might sound like for that activity. (See Appendix B for a copy of the guide.)

Example Activities

The following are examples of mathematical activities with built-in opportunities for students to use operation sense to generalize, in the sense of calculating without calculating and abstracting from computation.

A Long Sum

This first activity calls for using a calculating shortcut, providing practice with grouping numbers.

A Long Sum[4]

Find the value of the following:

$$1 - 2 + 3 - 4 + 5 - 6 + \ldots - 120$$

Notice that you can group the terms in this sum into pairs in several different ways. We might write the sum as $(1 - 2) + (3 - 4) + (5 - 6) + \ldots + (119 - 120)$. Then the problem reduces to calculating the sum of 60 negative ones. Alternatively, we could write the sum as $1 + (-2 + 3) + (-4 + 5) + \ldots + (-118 + 119) - 120$, which simplifies to $1 + 59 - 120 = -60$. The features of Abstracting from Computation are clearly at play here. (What are other ways to write that expression that will bring out hidden meaning? What are my operation shortcuts for getting from here to there?) As an extension, explore the sum $1 - 2 + 3 - 4 + \ldots + n$.

Number Lattices

This problem asks for a shortcut for doing an informal calculation. While the problem doesn't actually involve "calculating" in the usual sense of the word, with objects like numbers or variables, it does involve an informal kind of calculation that is not unlike the one earlier in this chapter.

Number Lattices[5]

In the following table, numbers in cells are related to other numbers by the arrow operations. If one number is given, what other numbers can you find? What values are at *A* and *B*? Can you find a shortcut that will take you from point *A* to point *B*? What if the down arrow was +2 instead of ×2?

If you are given one number in the lattice along with a rule, you can find the value of any other space in the lattice by working your way from the given number to the space in question by using the rules. In the example here, to get from the given number, 1500, to the space in question containing the A, move to the left once and divide by 5 to get $A = 300$. To calculate the value of B, given the value of A, we have many options. We can move our way from A to B by making a succession of downward or sideways moves; we would need six such moves. Alternatively, consider creating a new move, a *diagonal move*. (What are my operation shortcuts here?) What would moving diagonally toward the bottom and the right of the grid be equivalent to? If you can develop a rule to describe diagonal movement, you can get from A to B in just three steps. Regardless of your method, you should find that $B = 300,000$.

Try to construct some grids that follow the second rule, in which the down arrow is +2. How is this calculating situation like/unlike that one? Are the grids consistent? Suppose you are given a number and want to calculate the number in the space diagonal to it, down one unit and to the right one unit. Will you get the same answer regardless of whether you move down first (multiplying by 2) and then move to the right (adding 5) or move to the right first and then down? What does this tell you about the grid?

String of Pearls

This problem provides an opportunity to come up with calculating shortcuts that are a bit more hidden than in the previous two activities.

String of Pearls[6]

On a string of pearls, the largest pearl is in the center and the smallest pearls are on the ends. Each of the small pearls on the two ends costs $1; each of the next larger pearls costs $2 each; the third pearl from each end costs $3 each; and so on. On the basis of this plan, how much would a string of 9 pearls cost? 12? 25? n?

For a necklace with 7 pearls, the cost is figured by $1 + 2 + 3 + 4 + 3 + 2 + 1$. For 8 pearls, it is figured by $1 + 2 + 3 + 4 + 4 + 3 + 2 + 1$. (It is natural to relate this problem to the Sums of Consecutive Numbers problem that appears later in this problem set.) For the general case of n pearls, a way of expressing the sum 1 through n is $n(n + 1)/2$. (Computing this formula is not unlike what you did in the Long Sum problem.) So, if n is even, we need to compute the sum of 1 through $n/2$ and multiply that sum by 2. Using the formula, the sum is $(n/2)[(n/2) + 1]/2$, which equals $n(n + 2)/8$. Twice this is $n(n + 2)/4$. So, the answer for n even is $n(n + 2)/4$ dollars.

Similarly, you can show that, for n odd, a necklace with n pearls on the string costs $[(n + 1)/2]^2$ dollars. To do it, you need to think about what you just did in the case of n even and be guided by this question: How is this calculating situation like/unlike that one?

Proof

Set in a context different from the previous problems, this problem asks for reasoning to explain a given calculation. In the classroom, it can push students to go beyond mere computation, to recognize a pattern in a sum that will help them argue that the inequality holds.

Proof[7]

Prove that $1/2 < 1/101 + 1/102 + \ldots + 1/200 < 1$.

What are my operating shortcuts? One shortcut might be to use a couple of benchmarks, 1/200 and 1/100: "There are 100 terms in the sum, and each of the 100 terms in the sum is between 1/200 and 1/100 inclusive. If I have 100 fractions, each greater than 1/200, then their sum is going to be greater than 100 copies of 1/200, which equals 100/200, or 1/2." Similar reasoning can be used to show the other end of the inequality.

Weighing Meat

This activity develops number sense because it makes students think flexibly about how to generate 40 different numbers by adding and subtracting just four different values. Furthermore, this problem presents students with opportunities to calculate without calculating; there are connections that can be made among the various cases in this problem that result in calculational shortcuts.

Weighing Meat[8]

You have a balance scale, and you are trying to weigh 40 packages of meat ranging in weight from 1 kg to 40 kg. You have only four weights with which to work— a 1-kg, 3-kg, 9-kg, and 27-kg weight. How can you weigh each package of meat with just these four weights?

Look for shortcuts in finding solutions to this problem. Use previous work, when you can, to arrive at solutions.

First, the easy and obvious solutions:

1 kg of meat balances with the 1–kg weight.

3 kg of meat balance with the 3–kg weight.

9 kg of meat balance with the 9-kg weight.

27 kg of meat balance with the 27-kg weight.

A few less obvious solutions:

10 kg of meat balance with the 9-kg weight and the 1-kg weight.

11 kg of meat and the 1-kg weight balance with the 9-kg weight and the 3-kg weight.

12 kg of meat balance with the 9-kg weight and the 3-kg weight.

13 kg of meat balance with the 9-kg weight, the 3-kg weight, and the 1-kg weight.

14 kg of meat, the 9-kg weight, the 3-kg weight, and the 1-kg weight balance the 27-kg weight.

15 kg of meat, the 9-kg weight, and the 3-kg weight balance the 27-kg weight.

16 kg of meat, the 9-kg weight, and the 3-kg weight balance the 27-kg weight and the 1-kg weight.

17 kg of meat, the 9-kg weight, and the 1-kg weight balance the 27-kg weight.

18 kg of meat and the 9-kg weight, balance the 27-kg weight.

19 kg of meat and the 9-kg weight balance the 27-kg weight and the 1-kg weight.

20 kg of meat, the 9-kg weight, and the 1-kg weight balance the 27-kg weight and the 3-kg weight.

Figure the rest. Note that $40 = 1 + 3 + 9 + 27$ and that the four weights are powers of 3: 3^0, 3^1, 3^2, and 3^3. If we added a weight of $3^4 = 81$, could we get all weights up to $1 + 3 + 9 + 27 + 81 = 121$? Would this problem work if we replaced the numbers 1, 3, 9, and 27 with other numbers (e.g., 1, 3, 10, and 26)? Why or why not?

Putting the discussion into a more general context, this activity suggests combining monomials 1, x, x^2, x^3 with multiples of 0, −1, or 1, such as $1 - x$, $x + x^2$, and so on. Writing all such combinations, there are 81 (why?). Write out a number of these and factor; for example, $x + x^2 = x(1 + x)$. By doing so, you may see what is so special about the number 3.

High–Low Differences

This problem not only provides practice in looking for patterns in calculations and abstracting from those patterns to encourage calculating without calculating, but also provides an opportunity to become familiar with how the decimal system works. In classroom use, this problem requires students to use their understanding of the decimal system to explain why the patterns in this problem exist.

High–Low Differences[9]

In this problem, you will investigate a certain rule for generating a sequence of numbers. The rule involves the repeated use of a three-step arithmetic process. The following example shows how this three-step process works if you start with the number 473.

Step 1. Arrange the digits from largest to smallest: 743

Step 2. Arrange the digits from smallest to largest: 347

Step 3. Subtract the smaller number from the larger one: 743 – 347 = 396

The result of subtraction, 396, is called the *high–low difference* for the original number 473. You can then take 396 and find *its* high–low difference, and so on. We will call the numbers you get in this manner the *high–low sequence* for the starting number 473. Your task in this problem is to investigate these sequences for various three-digit starting numbers. You should continue with each high–low sequence until something interesting happens. Look for patterns in the high–low sequence and for reasons that explain what you see happening.

Eventually, all three-digit high–low sequences reach the number 495. What patterns are there in the sequences? For instance, starting with the second term in the sequence (in this case, 396), 9 is always the middle digit in the number, while the outside digits add up to 9. Furthermore, the outside digits of the numbers in the sequence follow their own pattern. As an extension, examine high–low sequences for numbers with four or more digits.

Differences of Squares

This problem also appeared in Chapter 3. We placed it in both chapters because it engages one's number sense for square numbers by requiring a search for patterns in the differences of squares; at the same time, it engages one's operation sense. See Chapter 3 for a discussion of the solution.

Differences of Squares

Which numbers can be expressed as the difference of two perfect squares?

Arithmagons

An alternate representation of a simple system of equations, this arithmagon allows for students to utilize intuitive, informal operation sense. It is accessible to students at all middle and high school grades.

Arithmagons[10]

What numbers can go in the circles so that the sum of each pair equals the number on the edge between them? How many solutions are there? Investigate what sets of three integers can be put on the edges, such that there are integer solutions.

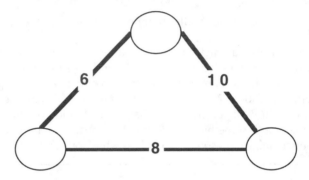

It is possible to see a connection between this and the middle-grades activity we highlighted in the earlier section, "A Thread of Algebraic Generalization." To see the connection, you might be guided by the following question: How is the calculating situation like/unlike that one? One answer to this guiding question is, "They are alike in that they involve equations with two unknowns in each; but the situations are different in that the total number of unknowns is three."

Try, as many students will, a guess-and-check approach to this. You should arrive at answers 2, 4, and 6. Like the numbers on the sides, these are even whole numbers. If you try three other even numbers on the sides, will the same thing happen? (When I do the same thing with different numbers, what still holds true? What changes?) For that matter, will any three whole numbers on the sides yield solutions? Will they always be whole number solutions? What other questions occur to you?

To get at the answers, it helps to analyze the situation algebraically. (What are other ways to write the expression to bring out hidden meaning?) The arithmagon, with sides a, b, and c and vertices x, y, and z, is a representation of the following system of equations:

$$x + y = a$$
$$x + z = b$$
$$y + z = c$$

So, one way to answer the question would be to solve the system of equations. When we do this, we find that $x = (a + b - c)/2; y = (a - b + c)/2; z = (-a + b + c)/2$. If we are working with arithmagons that have integer sides and we want solutions with integer vertices, we must have that $a + b - c, a - b + c,$ and $-a + b + c$ are even. This happens if either $a, b,$ and c are all even, or if exactly one of $a, b,$ and c is even.

The arithmagon can be helpful in the classroom because it organizes information contained in the foregoing system of equations in a different way, one that is more intuitive for some students. How do guess-and-check approaches used with the arithmagon relate to techniques used with equations?

Sums of Consecutive Numbers

This is a classic activity that pushes students to calculate without calculating, and teachers in our projects have used it productively with students from grades 6 through 10. In particular, Linked Learning teachers used it in their student interviews. Appendix B contains the interview guide for Sums of Consecutive Numbers.

Sums of Consecutive Numbers[11]

$$3 + 4 = 7$$

$$2 + 3 + 4 = 9$$

$$4 + 5 + 6 + 7 = 22$$

These problems are examples of sums of consecutive numbers. The number 7 is shown as the sum of two consecutive numbers. The number 9 is shown as the sum of three consecutive numbers. The number 22 is shown as the sum of four consecutive numbers. In this activity, you will explore what numbers can and cannot be made by sums of consecutive numbers.

1. For each number from 1 to 35, find all the ways to write it as a sum of two or more consecutive numbers.

2. What can you discover about sums of consecutive numbers? Explore and record three discoveries that you can share with the class.

3. Without doing any calculations, predict whether each of the following numbers can be made with two consecutive numbers, three consecutive numbers, four consecutive numbers, and so on. Explain why you made the predictions you did.

   a. 45

   b. 57

   c. 62

d. 75

e. 80

4. Use the discoveries you made in question 2 to come up with shortcuts for writing the following numbers as the sum of two or more consecutive numbers. Describe the shortcuts you created and tell how you used them to write each of the following numbers as sums of consecutive numbers.

a. 45

b. 57

c. 62

d. 75

e. 80

There are many ways to approach this problem. Someone with a bent to "calculate without calculating" will notice a symmetry in the sums she is computing; this symmetry can be capitalized on to avoid messy calculations. (How can I predict what's going to happen without doing all the calculations?)

For instance, suppose we wanted to calculate the following sum of consecutive numbers: $3 + 4 + 5 + 6 + 7$. We could go through the calculations directly, or we could notice that this sum has a symmetry to it. We rewrite the sum as $(5 - 2) + (5 - 1) + 5 + (5 + 1) + (5 + 2)$. This simplifies our calculation considerably; we see that the sum is equal to 5×5. Here we were able to calculate the sum without actually going through any laborious calculations. (How can I write the expression in terms of things I care about?)

Figuring out whether a given number can be written as the sum of n numbers is relatively straightforward when n is odd. Using reasoning similar to that just used, you can show that if n is odd, a number x can be written as the sum of n numbers if and only if n is a factor of x. If n is a factor of x, then we can represent the sum of consecutive numbers as follows: $[x/n - (n - 1)/2] + \ldots + (x/n - 2) + (x/n - 1) + x/n + (x/n + 1) + (x/n + 2) + \ldots + [x/n + (n - 1)/2]$. Try this with $x = 80$ and $n = 5$.

What about when n is even? (How is this calculating situation like/unlike that one?) Think about how you might use a similar strategy to calculate without calculating when n is even. For example, suppose you want to find the following sum: $5 + 6 + 7 + 8$. We could rewrite the sum in terms of 6 or 7 and eliminate some terms. Suppose we choose 6. Then the sum can be rewritten as follows: $(6 - 1) + 6 + (6 + 1) + (6 + 2)$. Writing the sum this way helps us to see that the sum is equal to $4 \times 6 + 2$. Alternatively, we could write this sum in terms of the number halfway between 6 and 7, the number 6.5. Then our sum becomes $(6.5 - 1.5) + (6.5 - 0.5) + (6.5 + 0.5) + (6.5 + 1.5)$. Writing the sum this way, we find a different way to calculate the sum, and we see that the sum is equal to 4×6.5. (What are other ways to write that expression that will bring out hidden meaning?)

Think about these two representations. How might you use them to figure out when a given number can be written as the sum of n numbers where n is even? The problem brings into play Doing–Undoing, in that it requires you to decide, for a given number, whether and how it can be decomposed into a sum of consecutive numbers. (Can I decompose this number or expression into helpful components?)

The Haybaler Problem

This problem calls for a different kind of number and operation sense than that called for in the previous problems. Number sense comes into play in the beginning of the problem, with questions about the relative weights of bales of hay. Operation sense is called into play to take advantage of some calculational shortcuts that are of a different nature than the calculational shortcuts taken in earlier problems.

The Haybaler Problem[12]

You have five bales of hay. For some reason, instead of being weighed individually, they were weighed in all possible combinations of two: bales 1 and 2, bales 1 and 3, bales 1 and 4, bales 1 and 5, bales 2 and 3, bales 2 and 4, and so on. The weights of each of these combinations were written down and arranged in numerical order, *without keeping track of which weight matched which pair of bales*. The weights in kilograms were 80, 82, 83, 84, 85, 86, 87, 88, 90, and 91. Your initial task is to find out how much each bale weighs. There may be more than one possible solution; if this is so, find out what all of the solutions are and explain how you know. Once you have finished looking for solutions, look back over the problem to see if you can find some easier or more efficient way to find the weights.

To begin this problem, you might consider the following questions. What can be said about the pair of bales that weighed the least? What must be the weights be of the two bales in this pair relative to the other bales of hay? What can be said about the pair of bales that weighed the most? What about the bales that weighed second to the lightest and second to the heaviest? Can anything helpful be said about them? What about the other pairs of bales? All of these questions elicit Doing–Undoing, with the guiding question, "Can I decompose this number or expression into helpful components?"

Asking and answering questions such as these should help to reveal a relationship between the lightest and second lightest (their combined weight is 80 kg), between the second lightest and third lightest (their weights differ by 2 kg), and so on, to a relationship between the lightest and the heaviest (their weights differ by 8 kg—why?) A key to this answer is to recognize that the third lightest is also the third heaviest, which mathematically elicits the guiding question, "What are other ways to write that expression that will bring out hidden meaning?"

After working through the problem, you should get that there is only one possible set of weights for the bales of hay: Their weights, in kilograms, are 39, 41, 43, 44, and 47.

Notes

1. The content is adapted from a series of activities in *Mathematics in Context: Comparing Quantities, Section B.* 1998. Chicago: Encyclopaedia Britannica Educational Corporation.
2. The example is drawn from a meeting of the six teams from the Assessment Communities of Teachers (ACT) Project in March of 1996.
3. This activity was developed by Eugene McCall, Jr., Milwaukee Public Schools.
4. This activity is from Bowers, H. & J. Bowers. 1961. *Arithmetical Excursions,* 231. New York: Dover.
5. This activity is adopted from materials developed by David Page for the University of Illinois Arithmetic Project in the 1960s. Materials from that project are available on the CD-ROM MathFINDER, available from The Learning Team, Armonk, New York.
6. Excerpted from "The Problem of Evaluation in Problem-Solving: Can We Find Solutions?" by W. Szetela, *Arithmetic Teacher,* 1987, Vol. 35, No. 3.
7. This activity is from Gelfand, I.M. & A. Shen. 1993. *Algebra.,* 127. Boston: Birkhauser.
8. From *Teaching Problem Solving Strategies,* by Dan Dolan and James Williamson. Copyright 1983 by Addison-Wesley Publishing Company. Reprinted by permission.
9. Excerpted from "The Overland Trail," *Interactive Mathematics Program Year 1,* copyright 1997 by Interactive Mathematics Program. Published by Key Curriculum Press (Emeryville, CA).
10. Adapted from Mason, J. 1996. "Expressing Generality and Roots of Algebra." In *Approaches to Algebra,* eds. N. Bednarz, C. Kieran & L. Lee, 78. Dordrecht: Kluwer Academic Publishers. With kind permission from Kluwer Academic Publishers.
11. This version of this activity was developed by EDC staff for professional development projects; the activity can be found in various materials, such as the *Interactive Mathematics Program.*
12. Excerpted from "The Overland Trail," *Interactive Mathematics Program Year 1,* copyright 1997 by Interative Mathematics Program. Published by Key Curriculum Press (Emeryville, CA).

References and Further Reading

Burrill, G. 1997. "Choices and Challenges." *Mathematics Teaching in the Middle School* 3: 92–96.

Curcio, F.R., B. Nimerofsky, R. Perez, & S. Yaloz. 1997. "Exploring Patterns in Nonroutine Problems." *Mathematics Teaching in the Middle School* 2: 262–69.

Education Development Center. 1992. *MathFINDER*. Armonk, NY: The Learning Team.

Friedlander, A. & R. Hershkowitz. 1997. "Reasoning with Algebra." *Mathematics Teacher* 90: 442–47.

McIntosh, A., R.E. Reys & B.J. Reys. 1997. "Mental Computation in the Middle Grades: The Importance of Thinking Strategies." *Mathematics Teaching in the Middle School* 2: 322–27.

Ruopp, F. et al. 1997. "Algebraic Thinking: A Theme for Professional Development." *Mathematics Teacher* 90: 150–54.

Wheeler, D. 1996. "Backwards and Forwards: Reflections on Different Approaches to Algebra." In *Approaches to Algebra*, eds. N. Bednarz, C. Kieran & L. Lee, 317–25. Dordrecht, The Netherlands: Kluwer Academic Publishers.

Appendix A: Example from Linear Algebra

Linear Algebra

In many ways, linear algebra is set in a context very different than the context of middle and high school algebra. Instead of dealing with the numbers, addition, and multiplication of middle and high school algebra, in linear algebra we deal with different objects (e.g., matrices) and different operations (e.g., matrix addition and multiplication). However, the systems are similar in that they each have a definite structure on which they are built. As students become comfortable with a system and its underlying structure, they begin to recognize patterns in calculations they perform and get a sense for how the objects in their system relate to one another.

We utilize operation sense and the calculating without calculating habit of mind in linear algebra when we use our understanding of the basic objects and operations of a system in linear algebra to find shortcuts to computations. For example, consider the proof of Cramer's Rule. In this proof, we rely on our familiarity with the determinant function to find a calculating shortcut that leads to an elegant proof.

Cramer's Rule is as follows. Suppose we are given an $n \times n$ matrix A, the determinant of which is not equal to 0, along with a column vector B with n components. We will write A and B as follows:

$$A = \begin{bmatrix} a_{11} & a_{12} & \cdots & a_{1n} \\ a_{21} & a_{22} & \cdots & a_{2n} \\ \vdots & \vdots & \ddots & \vdots \\ a_{n1} & a_{n2} & \cdots & a_{nn} \end{bmatrix} \quad B = \begin{bmatrix} b_1 \\ b_2 \\ \vdots \\ b_n \end{bmatrix}.$$

Now consider the system $AX = B$, where X is some unknown column vector. Write X as follows:

$$X = \begin{bmatrix} x_1 \\ x_2 \\ \vdots \\ x_n \end{bmatrix}.$$

Using matrix notation, the system with which we are working can be written

$$\begin{bmatrix} a_{11} & a_{12} & \cdots & a_{1n} \\ a_{21} & a_{22} & \cdots & a_{2n} \\ \vdots & \vdots & \ddots & \vdots \\ a_{n1} & a_{n2} & \cdots & a_{nn} \end{bmatrix} \begin{bmatrix} x_1 \\ x_2 \\ \vdots \\ x_n \end{bmatrix} = \begin{bmatrix} b_1 \\ b_2 \\ \vdots \\ b_n \end{bmatrix}.$$

Cramer's Rule gives us the solution to this system: It says that for all i, we have that $x_i = \det(B_i)/\det(A)$, where det represents the determinant function and B_i is the matrix we get when we replace the ith column in A with the column vector B. So, for example, we have that

$$B_1 = \begin{bmatrix} b_1 & a_{12} & a_{13} & \cdots & a_{1n} \\ b_2 & a_{22} & a_{23} & \cdots & a_{2n} \\ \vdots & \vdots & \vdots & \ddots & \vdots \\ b_n & a_{n2} & a_{n3} & \cdots & a_{nn} \end{bmatrix} \text{ and } B_2 = \begin{bmatrix} a_{11} & b_1 & a_{13} & \cdots & a_{1n} \\ a_{21} & b_2 & a_{23} & \cdots & a_{2n} \\ \vdots & \vdots & \vdots & \ddots & \vdots \\ a_{n1} & b_n & a_{n3} & \cdots & a_{nn} \end{bmatrix}.$$

To simplify notation later, let's introduce another way to notate the matrices B_i. For all i, let A_i represent the ith column in the matrix A. Then we can write $B_1 = (B, A_2, A_3, \ldots, A_n)$, $B_2 = (A_1, B, A_3, A_4, \ldots, A_n)$, and so on.

We will prove that the foregoing solution for x_i holds for $i = 1$; the proof for the general case follows the same reasoning. To prove that $x_i = \det(B_i)/\det(A)$, we have several options. We could calculate the determinants of the two matrices in question using methods such as Lagrange expansion, and hope that everything works out in the end. However, this would take a long time and be quite tedious. Instead, let us use what we know about objects, operations, and functions in this space to *look for a shortcut*; in doing this, we will use the habit of mind Abstracting from Computation.

To prove that $x_i = \det(B_i)/\det(A)$, it would be helpful to be able to calculate $\det(B_i)$. Recall that B_1 is the matrix whose first column is the column vector B and whose remaining $n - 1$ columns are the last $n - 1$ columns of the matrix A. Furthermore, we know that $B = AX$. So, we know that $\det(B_1) = \det(AX, A_2, A_3, \ldots, A_n)$. We will need to relate the vector AX to the matrix A and the vector X. We rely on our familiarity with this system to recall an elementary theorem in linear algebra: $AX = x_1 A_1 + x_2 A_2 + \ldots x_n A_n$. Furthermore, based on our *operation sense* in this context, we intuit that complication of the vector $AX =$ into the expression $x_1 A_1 + x_2 A_2 + \ldots + x_n A_n$ will help us find the shortcut for which we are looking (thus being guided by this question: How can I write the expression in terms of things I care about?)

If we substitute this sum for the column vector B when we calculate $\det(B_1)$, we get $\det(B_1) = \det(B, A_2, A_3, \ldots, A_n) = \det(x_1 A_1 + x_2 A_2 + \ldots + x_n A_n, A_2, A_3, \ldots, A_n)$.

Although this looks complicated, we recognize, based on our knowledge of and familiarity with the determinant function, that the problem is now more approachable. A person familiar with the determinant function knows that it is linear and capitalizes on this linearity. We *reason by linearity* when we notice that, because the determinant function is linear, we have

$$\det(x_1 A_1 + x_2 A_2 + \ldots + x_n A_n, A_2, A_3, \ldots, A_n) = x_1 \det(A_1, A_2, \ldots, A_n) + x_2 \det(A_2, A_2, \ldots, A_n) + x_3 \det(A_3, A_2, \ldots, A_n) \ldots + x_n \det(A_n, A_2, \ldots, A_n).$$

We can now employ one last property of the determinant function: The determinant of a matrix with two identical rows is equal to 0. In the foregoing sum, the second through the nth terms will then be equal to 0, because in each term, we are taking the determinant of such a matrix. For example, in the second term in the foregoing sum, we take the determinant of a matrix, the first two columns of which are identical to A_2. In the third term in the foregoing sum, we take the determinant of a matrix, the first and third columns of which are identical to A_3, and so on. Hence, except for the first term in the sum, all of the terms in the foregoing sum are equal to 0. Furthermore, because $(A_1, A_2, \ldots, A_n)$ is just another way to write the matrix A, we have that $\det(B_1) = x_1 \det(A)$. We need only divide by $\det(A)$ to get the result we sought to prove. In the statement of Cramer's Rule, we know that the determinant of A is nonzero, so we do not need to worry about dividing by zero.

In this proof, knowledge of the properties of the objects, operations, and functions in the context of matrix algebra resulted in finding a *calculational shortcut*. Using this understanding of the structure of a system to come up with shortcuts is part of what constitutes using the habit of mind Abstracting from Computation. Just as in middle and high school algebra we avoid a messy calculation by recognizing a general pattern among the numbers and operations with which we are calculating, in linear algebra we do a similar thing, except that we do it with different objects and operations. We calculate with things such as matrices and the determinant function. Knowing how these objects and functions relate, we find shortcuts to performing otherwise long and tedious calculations. It is important to push students toward developing this generalized ability to recognize patterns in calculations, because it is omnipresent in all of mathematics.

Appendix B: LLMP Guide for Student Interviews

We have put together some suggestions to help you focus on your students' algebraic thinking as you try to conduct, listen, and analyze their interviews. The examples here are related to your students' work on the Sums of Consecutive Numbers activity. However, these examples can be applied to the other interviews as well. We have listed a few questions to guide your listening, along with some features of student algebraic thinking that you may find helpful. They relate to the three habits of mind we have followed in Linked Learning, although they are organized a bit differently: We put some references to *Doing–Undoing* under *Building Rules to Represent Functions* and some under *Abstracting from Computation*. This is because it is a habit of mind that serves well for working with functions and for working with number expressions. In addition, some aspects of generalization are listed under *Building Rules to Represent Functions*, and other aspects of generalization are listed under *Abstracting from Computation*. Again, this is because you might hear a generalization about a functional rule or you might hear a generalization about an expression or calculation. Finally, we list some features of convincing argument that can apply to both *Building . . .* and *Abstracting . . . .*

Following is the list of questions and related features. *However, not every interview needs to elicit all of these points.* The examples contain suggestions of how the referenced feature could appear in the context of Sums of Consecutive Numbers.

Building Rules to Represent Functions

Overarching question: *What do these students know about building rules to represent functions?* In listening for evidence, you may notice some of the following, which are listed roughly in increasing order of sophistication:

1. Generates cases and compares them systematically, searching for a rule.

    Example: "I've been comparing all the numbers I generated that are the sums of three consecutive numbers, and they're all divisible by 3."

2. Attempts to describe a rule verbally, with reference to how the rule works.

    Example: "To find out if a number can be written as the sum of five consecutive numbers, look to see if it ends in a 5 or a 0."
    Example: "To get the sum of five consecutive numbers that start with 3, add 5 to the sum that starts with 2." (*This describes a recursive rule.*)

3. Conjectures a rule.

    Example: "From the pattern in the table it looks like the sum of three consecutive numbers will always be 3 times the first number plus 3."

4. Represents this rule in other forms:

Table

Graph

Equation   *Example:* Sum $= 10 + 5f$, where f is first number

Expression   *Example:* $10 + 5f$, where f is first number

5. Links are made among the different representations to show how they connect.

   Example: "The 5 in the formula means if the starting number gets bigger by 1, the sum gets bigger by 5."

6. Shows it is possible to go from output back to input.

   Example: "If you give me the sum of three consecutive numbers, all I have to do is subtract 3, then divide by 3, and that will give me the starting number." (*undoing*)

7. Generalizations made about rule:

   a. Predictions are made about what is true about the rule or about how the rule will extend.

      Example: "The rule will work even if the numbers are negative."

   b. Consideration is given to other cases for which the rule works.

      Example: "The rule will work for the sum of seven consecutive numbers . . ."

   c. Consideration is given to *all* the cases for which the rule works.

      Example: "The rule will work for the sum of any odd number of consecutive numbers . . ."

8. To undo, the equation derived by the student is rewritten and solved.

   Example: "$50 = 10 + 5f$. Subtract 10 from both sides: $40 = 5f$. Divide both sides by 5: $8 = f$. 8 is the first number. The consecutive numbers are $8 + 9 + 10 + 11 + 12$."

Abstracting from Computation

Overarching question: *What do these students know about abstracting from computation?* In listening for evidence, you may notice some of the following, which are listed roughly in increasing order of sophistication:

1. Tries calculating a result in another case to see if it works.

   Example: "If a sum of five consecutive whole numbers is the same as five times the middle number, I wonder if the same kind of thing happens with *seven* consecutive numbers."

2. Generalizes about computation:

   a. Uses calculating shortcuts that seem to reveal an understanding of how the number system works.

      Example: "A sum of five consecutive whole numbers is the same as five times the middle number . . ." (*a form of generalizing*)

   b. Conjectures a calculating result to be true independent of the particular numbers used.

      Example: "No matter where the starting number is, to get the sum of four consecutive numbers, just add 6 on to four times the starting number— like 9 + 10 + 11 + 12 is 4 × 9 + 6." (*a form of generalizing*)

3. Works backward to "undo" numbers, for example, recognizing that a particular number fits a particular expression.

   Example: "34 can be expressed as a sum of four consecutive numbers because it fits the form $4n + 6$, with 7 as n." (*undoing*)

4. Rewrites number expressions to bring out possibly helpful features.

   Example: "Instead of writing the consecutive numbers 10, 11, 12, 13, we can write them as 10, 10 + 1, 10 + 2, 10 + 3."

Convincing Argument

These features of convincing arguments can be applied to Building Rules or Abstracting from Computation. In either case, students who make convincing arguments within either of those types show a higher level of algebraic thinking.

Overarching question: *What do these students know about making convincing arguments?* In listening for evidence, you may notice some of the following, which are listed roughly in increasing order of sophistication:

1. Challenge one another to build a rule, abstract from computation, or convince others why something works.

   Example: "That's a really neat pattern. Let's figure out why it happens and find a rule that generates it."

2. Explains *how* their rule or calculation worked.

   Example: "See, I take the first number, 6, and multiply it by 5 to get 30. Then I add 10 and get 40."

3. Connects their explanations back to the original context of the problem.

   Example: "Let's see. The problem asked me which numbers can be written as sums of consecutive numbers and in how many ways, but I've only answered for odd numbers."

4. Makes a distinction between *conjecturing* what is true about the rule and *establishing* what is true about the rule.

    Example: "From the pattern in the table it looks like the sum of three consecutive numbers will always be 3 times the first number plus 3, but how can I be sure that will always be true?"

5. Explains why their rule or calculation worked, or *why* their generalization worked.

    Example: "The reason the sum of the five consecutive numbers is the same as 5 times the middle number is that middle number is the average of the five numbers. Since the average is the sum divided by 5, then average times 5 must be the sum."

Conclusion

Remember that the main purpose of the interview is for you to get more familiar with students' thinking in some areas that we believe are key to algebra proficiency. This is an opportunity for you to keep your eyes and ears open for anything you find interesting regarding algebraic thinking. This also is an opportunity to try doing some things you may not do in the classroom. For example, if it seems that the students are stuck, wait a bit before you say anything—at least a half minute or so—in order to see whether they get themselves unstuck.

When you write about the interviewing, here are some questions to which you can attend:

What do these students know about building rules to represent functions (or about abstracting from computation)?

What evidence do I have in what they did or said?

What are my best guesses about the thinking that was behind what they did or said?

What surprised me about the algebraic thinking that went on?

What am I left wondering about regarding the algebraic thinking that went on?

Last, but not least, we hope you and your students enjoy the interview experience.

5 Expressing Generalizations About Functional Relations

Introduction

The high visibility of pattern-based activities in recent school mathematics materials points to the increased value placed on teaching patterns as a productive way to introduce algebra. As early as kindergarten, students see colored geometric shapes, sequenced in orderly fashion; for a particular sequence, after five or six that have been shown to them, they may be asked to predict the next shape. Later, when number sense becomes a point of emphasis in the classroom, students are expected to recognize and describe various number-sequence patterns. Judging from conversations with numerous teachers in our projects and elsewhere, "Do you see a pattern?" is a commonly asked question in classrooms from elementary school on. Unfortunately, just as common are student difficulties in describing patterns in sufficiently general terms and in justifying their generalizations.

Two features of pattern work recommend it as a foundation for prealgebra and algebra, and as a way to foster algebraic thinking:

- First, it can serve students' learning about functional relations, and so ground their understanding of the concept of function, which some consider the fundamental algebraic concept (Schwartz & Yerushalmy 1992). For example, facility with functions is in the background as an important learning goal when students gather data, construct tables to represent the data, and then develop and test rules to see if their tables have predictive potential, as in:

Time in Months	Plant Height in Inches
1	5
2	7
3	9
4	11
.	.
.	.

In seeing the pattern, "For every increase of 1 month, the height increases by 2 inches," a student is on the way to a facility with linear functions, but, as teachers know, there is a lot of cognitive ground between seeing this pattern and understanding linear functions. One key hurdle is the students' difficulties in constructing a rule that "always works" for a linear relation like this one, in the sense that, given any number month, the rule can churn out the plant height for that month.

Other functional relationships besides linear relations are important in introductory algebra and, generally, they too are based on arithmetic computations, like the relation between a number and 3 times that number plus 1, or the one that relates a number to the number squared, or the one that relates a number to 2 raised to that number as a power. There are other kinds of functional relations in mathematics, such as those seen in trigonometry [e.g., $x \rightarrow \sin(x)$]. For each of these kinds of functions, some fundamental questions are, "What patterns and other characteristics set one kind of function apart from another kind?" and "For a particular kind of function, what is always true?"

- The habit of thinking that causes one to look beyond a perceived pattern to wonder what "always works" for the pattern's mathematical rule is a feature of a broader capacity of mathematical thinking: the recognition, expression, and manipulation of generalities, commonly called *generalization*. Generalization is a thinking process that applies throughout mathematics. In our work with algebraic thinking, not all generalizations build on students' informal understanding of functional relations. Some arise from a deep familiarity with calculation and the capacity to generalize from patterns seen in calculating contexts. For example,

1. Sums of consecutive powers of 2 reveal a pattern:

    $1 + 2 + 4 = 7$

    $1 + 2 + 4 + 8 = 15$

    $1 + 2 + 4 + 8 + 16 = 31$, etc., leading to a general statement:

    $$1 + 2 + 4 + 8 + \ldots + 2^n = 2^{n+1} - 1$$

2. Differences of consecutive perfect squares also reveal a pattern:

    $4 - 1 = 3$

    $9 - 4 = 5$

    $16 - 9 = 7$

    $25 - 16 = 9$, leading to a general statement relating consecutive perfect squares to consecutive odd numbers:

    $$n^2 - (n - 1)^2 = 2n - 1$$

3. Differences of consecutive unit fractions reveal yet another pattern:

$$1/2 - 1/3 = 1/2 \times 1/3$$

$$1/3 - 1/4 = 1/3 \times 1/4$$

$1/4 - 1/5 = 1/4 \times 1/5$, leading to the general statement:

$$1/n - 1/(n + 1) = 1/n \times 1/(n + 1)$$

The generalizations growing from such pattern recognition connect to the habit of mind we call Abstracting from Computation, those insights about the way computational operations work, which lead to observations and conclusions independent of particular numbers chosen. These kinds of generalization, evidence of a sort of *operation sense*, are the focus of Chapter 4. We touch on them in this chapter, but primarily the chapter covers the generalization challenges to middle and high school students and teachers around the *functional relations* encountered in algebra. Just as in Chapter 4, we will see that much of the challenge arises from the logical demands associated with generalization, that is, the need to *justify*, with logical reasoning, any generalized conclusions. Without justification, all one has to work with is conjecture. Thus, in the foregoing example, it is one thing to be able to express the generalization about consecutive unit fractions as $1/n - 1/(n + 1) = 1/n \times 1/(n + 1)$; it is quite another to show why this is more than conjecture, that it "always works."

Difficulties of Generalization

The full role of generalization in the development of algebraic thinking is beyond the scope of this chapter. Instead, our attention is given to aspects of generalization that are revealed in the guiding questions, which we have heeded in our several projects and which we introduced in Chapter 1—questions that simulate how algebraic thinking habits of mind are activated. For example, questions associated with the habit we call Building Rules to Represent Functions include questions aimed at generalizing:

- When I do the same thing with different numbers, what still holds true? What changes?

- Is there information here that lets me predict what's going to happen?

- Does my rule work for all cases?

- Am I doing the same steps over and over? What are they?

- Can I write down a mechanical rule that will do this job once and for all?

- How can I describe the steps without using specific inputs?

We want students, from middle school through high school, to habituate such lines of thinking. Instead, they often fall victim to a variety of pitfalls that stand in the way of good habits of generalizing. For example, following are pitfalls that present particular instructional challenges to teachers:

- **Students may generalize too quickly.** A common aspect of this phenomenon is captured by Mason (1996): "Unfortunately, there is . . . an established practice of making a table, guessing a formula, checking that it works on one or two more examples, and then moving on to the next question" (76). The associated challenge for teachers is how to move beyond the question "Do you see a pattern?" to holding students to age-appropriate standards for justifying statements about what is "always" true for a particular set of data.

- **Pattern spotting can remain trivial.** One activity we have used in our projects, called The Postage Stamp problem, includes the question "Suppose the post office has only 3-cent and 6-cent stamps. What combinations of postage are possible to make?" Some students make a table of various combinations, then look at what they have and decide that they see a pattern: All the postage amounts are multiples of 3. This is an empirical decision, based on what the table tells them, not on looking at the relationship between 3 and 6. If the numbers were changed to 5 and 10, it isn't clear whether they would have to make another table to see that all amounts are multiples of 5. This is a difficult phenomenon for teachers to navigate, because *trivial* can be a relative term. For younger students, who haven't yet internalized the distributive property, it may not be clear that combinations of 3 and 6 are multiples of 3; however, at some point in students' mathematical development, it would be inappropriate to let students rely on empirical pattern spotting without analyzing the underlying reasons that the numbers behave the way they do.

- **Students can generalize about the wrong properties.** As an example, this appears to happen for many students around the concept of function. Harel and Tall (1991) describe the phenomenon this way: "So difficult is this abstract concept that it seems not possible to present it in a sufficiently generic manner. Instead we see that pupils presented with an informal introduction to the function concept develop a menagerie of examples from which they abstract inappropriate properties" (40). In our projects, we have seen cases in which students inappropriately conclude, "This is a case of linear relation." For example, recall that in the activity from Chapter 1, called The Locker problem, students were first presented with the situation in which there are 20 lockers, then with the situation in which there are 200 lockers. See the questions asked in this activity.

The Locker Problem

In the case of 20 lockers, which lockers are still open after the twentieth student is finished? Which locker or lockers changed the most?

Suppose there are 200 lockers. Which lockers are open after the 200th student is finished? Which locker or lockers changed the most?

Some students correctly figure that, for each locker number, they need to look at the number of factors it has, to determine how many times the locker changes. When they do this for the 20-locker case, they correctly conclude that 12, 18, and 20 are the numbers with the most factors (six apiece). Then, when asked to shift to the 200-locker case, they assume that proportionality is relevant and conclude without checking that 120, 180, and 200 are the numbers with the most factors. This appears to be a case of inappropriately expecting the relation $n \rightarrow$ (number of factors of n) to be linear. A challenge for teachers, therefore, is to find ways for students to reveal the various properties they are attending to as they generalize.

Two Aspects of Generalization

This list of difficulties is not comprehensive, but it suggests two aspects of generalization that teachers may want to address in their efforts to understand and foster students' algebraic thinking, which we informally label as follows:

1. **Globalizing,** especially making the leap to what is "always true" for a functional relation

2. **Extending,** especially wondering about and pursuing the mathematical directions that an algebraic result may suggest, beyond the result itself

Globalizing

Over the past few years, we have heard from teachers in our projects how challenging it is to help students learn how to follow through on work on functional relations, not only to look for patterns and conjecture rules, but also to craft convincing arguments that the rules work for all relevant cases. We call this kind of following through *globalizing*—thinking about the "always" in considering mathematical rules and relations.

Friedlander and Hershkowitz (1997) suggest a way to scaffold activities to encourage globalizing, progressing from what they call a "working generalization" to an "explicit generalization":

- Show several examples of a generalizable phenomenon, such as

    $4 \times 4 = 16$ and $3 \times 5 = 15$

    $5 \times 5 = 25$ and $4 \times 6 = 24$

    $8 \times 8 = 64$ and $7 \times 9 = 63$

- Discuss what is common to these.

- Have students produce some additional examples of the "same kind."

- Give the students some large-number cases, such as $256 \times 256 = 65{,}536$. What is the product of 255×257?

- Have them try some "undoing," e.g., $16 \times 16 = 256$; __ $\times$ __ $= 255$?

- Ask students to find a general rule that applies to all of the foregoing exercises.

- Ask students to show that the rule is always true.

An Example of Globalizing

Globalizing can occur when students take the step from calculating inputs and outputs without noticing common relationships among them to seeing a pattern in a functional relation and coming up with a rule that expresses this pattern, a rule that they can justify. For instance, suppose students are looking at the following problem (seen in a different version in Chapter 1):

Toothpick Squares[1]

Shown below is a pattern of "growing" squares made from toothpicks.

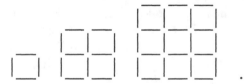

Find a rule that will let you find the number of toothpicks in any square in the above sequence.

Students begin to generalize when they consolidate their observations about the relationships among the numbers into a general statement. Depending on the approach to this problem, students will generalize in different ways. Here are two:

1. Tabular Approach

Some students will make a table similar to the following one:

Number of Toothpicks on Side of Square	Total Number of Toothpicks in Square
1	4
2	12
3	24
4	40
. . .	. . .

From here, several different forms of generalizing statements can arise. Some students might say that the numbers in the right-hand column increase in such a way that each increase is 4 more than the previous increase (i.e., increases of 8, 12, 16, . . .). In this case, the students are paying attention to change in the vertical direction, and they make the move from the particular to the general when they see and articulate the pattern in the increases in the right-hand column. (They are guided by these questions: How are things changing? How is this number related to the one that came before?)

Others will compare numbers in a horizontal direction. They might notice a computational relationship between the number of toothpicks on a side of a square of length n and the total number of toothpicks in the square. Their thinking is being guided by these questions: Am I doing the same steps over and over? What are they? Can I write down a mechanical rule that will do this job once and for all? How can I describe the steps without using specific inputs? Although a concise symbolic representation of the rule—for example, $n \rightarrow 2n(n + 1)$—may not arise, some computational connection may be noticed between the left and right sides. (For example, see the student work in an upcoming section, "Encouraging Generalization in the Classroom.") In this case, students make the generalizing step when they see the commonality among the relationships between numbers in each pair in the foregoing table and can state that commonality precisely.

No matter which way students choose to approach the data in the table, their results are similar: The students will have organized the information in the table into a system that allows them to calculate the number of toothpicks in a square of any length (however laborious that procedure might be). Eventually, we would like students to be able to pay attention to what is happening both vertically and horizontally in the table and to describe each.

Because of the nature of functional relations, students see patterns in functional relations in two major ways. Many students see and describe patterns recursively where outputs of functions are related to one another. Other students describe relations in closed functional terms, relating the input to the output. For example, in the Toothpick Squares activity, students of the former type pay attention to change in the vertical direction on the table, noticing that each increase is 4 more than in the previous increase. Others of the latter type notice change in the horizontal direction: They see that the number of toothpicks on a side of a square can be multiplied by one more than itself and then be doubled to get the total number of toothpicks in the square. To reach a deeper understanding of the underlying mathematics, it is important that students see functional relations in both of these ways and connect the two ways of seeing patterns to each other.

It is difficult for many students to move from the recursive representation to the closed functional representation. Accustomed to noticing patterns in strings of numbers (from their elementary school years), students are required to describe these patterns in a different way once they reach algebra. Describing relations recursively is highly valuable; after all, this kind of facility with recursion is key to understanding later mathematics, wherein students will encounter concepts such as difference functions in discrete mathematics. However, recursive descriptions of patterns are not sufficient as a preparation for equations work in algebra, for which a global and closed representation is needed, so some effort needs to be made to bridge the two ways of representing patterns.

2. Nontabular Approach

Some students will approach the Toothpick Squares problem without using a table, instead relying on visual organization and counting methods. They are attending to different information to answer the following guiding questions: Is there information here that lets me predict what's going to happen? How can I describe the steps without using specific inputs? For example, they might attempt to draw some squares and devise a counting scheme that will help them count toothpicks efficiently in the general case. For instance, consider the following counting system that can easily be used to count in the general case. Given a square with n toothpicks on each side, divide the toothpicks into two categories: the toothpicks on the outside border of the square and the toothpicks on the inside. The following diagram gives a visual representation of this concept for squares with 1, 2, and 3 toothpicks on a side. The toothpicks on the outside (in the first category) are represented by solid lines; the toothpicks on the inside (in the second category) are represented by dashed lines.

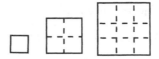

Dividing the counting in this visual manner (a form of undoing) helps in counting the toothpicks in the general case. For a square with n toothpicks on a side, there are $4n$ toothpicks on the outside, because there are n toothpicks on each of the 4 sides of the square. The inside of the square contains $2n(n-1)$ toothpicks, because there are $n-1$ columns of vertical toothpicks, each of which contains n toothpicks and $n-1$ rows of horizontal toothpicks, each of which contains n toothpicks. Add $4n$ and $2n(n-1)$ to get the total number of toothpicks in the square. When students approach the problem in this manner, their generalizing is visual before it is numerical, because they notice that this way of organizing interior rows and columns works for any square and can describe how to count in the general case. Like the students using a table, they have attended to this question: Does my rule cover all possible cases?

Extending

Another way in which a mathematical thinker can generalize is by *extending*, or following the lines of further inquiry suggested by a particular mathematical result. One productive way to encourage extending is to look at a mathematical statement and ask, "What if I changed . . . ?" about different mathematical features of the statement. For example, "What if I changed from two-dimensions to three-dimensions?" This "what-if" technique is described in Brown and Walter (1983).

An Example of Extending

Geometric patterns (like the Toothpick Squares problem) are a common feature of today's curriculum materials, and they can be used as a context in which to encourage students to extend their thinking—provided they are used in a way that encourages flexible thinking by students. Encouraging flexible thinking seems important. Lee (1996) summarizes a set of student interviews on geometric patterns by reporting, "seeing a useful pattern . . . seemed to be more of a problem than simply 'seeing a pattern.' Perceptual agility seemed to be a key: being able to see several patterns and willing to abandon those that do not prove useful" (95). Lee goes on to suggest that "pedagogically, the question of 'seeing a pattern' might be supplanted by 'seeing patterns,' teaching perceptual agility" (95).

The Brown and Walter technique is one way to foster such flexible thinking and extending. Applying the technique to the Toothpick Squares activity, teacher and students can extend the activity by asking the following:

- What if we only count the toothpicks inside the squares?

- What if the shape is changed to a nonsquare rectangle?

- What if we include diagonals?

- What about other geometric shapes?

- What if we go to higher dimensions?

Another Example of Extending

Drawing from a set of descriptions by Lee (1996), the following sequence of challenges to students, played out over time, can help them do some generalizing by extension. The extensions, which touch on both Building Rules to Represent Functions and Abstracting from Computation, first correspond to "What if the number changes?" then to "What if the operation changes?" The early challenges are accessible to middle and high school students; the later ones may be appropriate for high school students only. Several of the challenges are addressed later in this chapter:

Challenge 1: Show that the sum of any two consecutive whole numbers is an odd number.

Challenge 2: What can you say about the sum of three consecutive numbers?

Challenge 3: What can you say about the sum of four consecutive numbers?

Challenge 4: What can you say about the sum of n consecutive numbers?

Challenge 5:   What numbers can be written as the sum of consecutive integers?

Challenge 6:   What is the sum of n terms of an arithmetic progression (a sequence of numbers in which each term is the sum of the preceding term and a fixed number)?

Challenge 7:   What can you say about three consecutive multiples of a number n?

Challenge 8:   What is the sum of n terms of a geometric progression (a sequence of numbers in which each term is the product of the preceding term and a fixed number)?

Encouraging Generalization in the Classroom

A Role for Teacher Questions

To see how teachers might use algebraic-thinking questions to encourage students to think globally, consider the following piece of student work on the Toothpick Activity. (This sample also appeared in Chapter 1.) The student had drawn a picture of the 4×4 case, next to the 1×1, 2×2, and 3×3 drawings provided. Figure 5–1 is the student's entire response to question 5.

The student is apparently headed in a fruitful direction; it appears that she has begun to see a relationship between the number of toothpicks on a side and the total number of toothpicks in a square: For each of the four cases in Figure 5–1, it seems the student has found that the total number of toothpicks in a square is equal to the product of the number of toothpicks on each side of the square and the corresponding number in parentheses. This student is apparently missing the globalizing step in which she is able to express the underlying pattern in general terms. What questions could be asked of this student to push her to generalize? The following are some that come to mind: "When it says 'rule,' what does that mean to you?" "What would the next one look like?" "How did you get the number in the parentheses?" "How are the numbers in parentheses changing?" "What would be in the parentheses at the tenth step? the twentieth step?"

FIGURE 5–1.   *Student's Response to Question 5*

1-4(4)
2-12(6)
3-24(8)
4-46 (10)

We believe one type of question, asked on a regular basis in the classroom, can help students think through, articulate, and justify the rules they come up with—and so to globalize. These are questions tied to the algebraic habit of mind called Doing–Undoing, asking students if particular numbers can be outputs for the rules they have. For the student in the preceding example, these questions might be appropriate: "Can a large square have a total of 210 toothpicks? Why or why not?"

A study of sixth-graders' use of equations to describe and represent problem situations offers some insight on how to bridge the gap between thinking recursively and thinking functionally (Langrall & Swafford 1997). The study suggested that, to help students move from local and/or recursive descriptions of the patterns they see in tables to global and/or closed descriptions (e.g., in the form of equations), teachers should (1) have students work with a variety of numbers, large and small, in the tables (rather than let them leap to a conclusion from a few easy examples); and (2) have students "undo," as in, "Can 250 be an output on your table?" These are both components of the "working generalization" described earlier. Having students do this appears to focus them more clearly on the processes involved, thus making it easier to come up with representations of functional relationships.

Furthermore, teachers can help students who are having difficulty moving from thinking recursively to thinking functionally by showing them how to link what they *do* understand—recursive descriptions—to what they are struggling with—closed functional descriptions. For example, consider the following activity, which Linked Learning teachers did with their classes.

Towering Numbers[2]

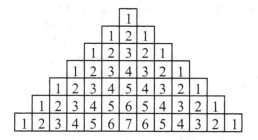

1. There are seven rows in the tower pictured above. How many bricks are in the seventh row?

2. Suppose you wanted to build a tower with 25 rows using the same design. Describe how you could figure out how many bricks you would need for the twenty-fifth (longest) row.

3. A very large tower was built using the same design. The longest row had 299 bricks in it. How many rows of bricks did the tower have?

4. If somebody told you how many rows of bricks were in a tower, how could

you figure out the number of bricks in the longest row?

5. If somebody told you how many bricks were in the longest row of a tower, how could you figure out how many rows there were?

For the most part, students in Linked Learning classrooms noticed that to find the number of bricks in a given row, they could add 2 to the number of bricks in the previous row. However, many students struggled to come up with a closed form of this relationship.

To help students move from this recursive description to a functional one, teachers can capitalize on students' understanding of the recursive relationship and use tables to build a closed form of a rule. First students can create a table relating the quantities with which they are dealing; in this case, students' tables would relate the number of rows to the number of bricks in the longest row:

Number of Rows	Number of Bricks in Longest Row
1	1
2	3
3	5
4	7
5	9
. . .	. . .

Then students can rewrite the right-hand column in ways that highlight the recursive relationship that has been found. In the Towering Numbers problem, students might go through a few stages of rewriting.[3] First, they might rewrite the number of bricks in the longest row in a form that makes explicit the "+2" recursive relationship between outputs already found:

Number of Rows	Number of Bricks in Longest Row	Number of Bricks in Longest Row (Long Way)
1	1	1
2	3	1 + 2
3	5	1 + 2 + 2
4	7	1 + 2 + 2 + 2
5	9	1 + 2 + 2 + 2 + 2
. . .	. . .	. . .

Once students have written the number of bricks in the longest row in this format, different patterns become more obvious. Each entry is equal to one more than a sum of 2s; what changes from row to row is the number of 2s in the sum. Students can then add a fourth column to their table, in which they write the numbers in the second and third columns in a form that reflects this observation:

Number of Rows	Number of Bricks in Longest Row	Number of Bricks in Longest Row (Long Way)	Number of Bricks in Longest Row (Short Way)
1	1	1	$1 + (0 \times 2)$
2	3	$1 + 2$	$1 + (1 \times 2)$
3	5	$1 + 2 + 2$	$1 + (2 \times 2)$
4	7	$1 + 2 + 2 + 2$	$1 + (3 \times 2)$
5	9	$1 + 2 + 2 + 2 + 2$	$1 + (4 \times 2)$
. . .	. . .	. . .	. . .

By the time students are at the stage of writing the last column, the closed form of the functional relationship is more clear. It is easier to see that for any number of rows, the number of bricks in the longest row will be 1 plus twice the quantity: number of rows minus 1.

This strategy can be used to help students form functional rules from recursive rules and link up the two descriptions, so that they see the relationship between, in this case, the "+2" in the recursive relationship and the "×2" in the functional relationship.

Encouraging Extending in the Classroom

In our earlier list of extension challenges to students, challenge 1—"Show that the sum of any two consecutive whole numbers is an odd number"—has proved difficult for students to justify. In one study involving 15-year-olds (Lee & Wheeler 1987), about half of the students were able to approach it symbolically, writing a, $a + 1$ as the two numbers and $2a + 1$ as the sum. From here, various manipulations, such as substitution, were tried, but few students were able to conclude from this that the sum is odd. They appeared to want to set $2a + 1$ *equal* to something. Writing about the study, Bell (1995) wrote that "the central purpose of algebra was perceived by these students as the performance of some manipulation; its use as a mode of expression of some generalizations . . . was absent" (46).

A similar observation was made in Chapter 4 about the difficulty students can have with the use of algebraic expressions as statements of generality rather than as components of equations. A teacher in our LUMR project brought to a team meeting a piece of student work (Figure 5–2) for a version of challenge 5: Students were asked to see how many numbers between 1 and 35 could be written as sums of consecutive numbers and to write about any patterns they noticed. The student's statement that "$n + 1 =$ odd always" seems to show confusion in using expressions as statements of generality.

Despite the fact that some (especially, younger) students may not be able to give a formal, symbolic proof for challenges such as challenge 1, there should be some effort—for it and the other challenges—to go beyond the empirical explanation, "It works for all the cases I've tried." Students may, for example, be able to come up with a verbal proof, such as, "If I add a number to the next number, I'm going to get two of the first number plus one, and that has to be odd." Again from

When you add an even and an odd you gang to end up with an odd answer.

When you add 2 evens to an odd you'll end up on an odd when you add to odds to an even you end up on an even

Formulas

$n+1 = $ odd always

a four numbered sequence

$=$ Sums
$n+n+1+n+2+n+3 = 5$

net $n = 0$

$n+1+n+2+n+3+n+4 = 5+4$

the LUMR project, a student gave the response in Figure 5–3 as part of the answer to challenge 5, which shows that students need not be using symbolic expressions to express generality well. As a matter of fact, the student overgeneralized, offering a way to express any even number as a sum of four consecutive numbers. What the student did offer, however, works for even numbers that are not powers of 2.

Encouraging Convincing Arguments in the Classroom

As one of their professional development activities, teachers in the Linked Learning project had been interviewing three of their students over the course of the year, looking for indicators of algebraic thinking. They had been looking, in particular, for signs of generalization and convincing argument as the students worked

FIGURE 5–3. *Student Work Showing Generality*

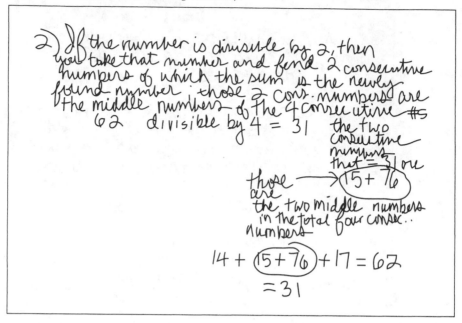

on mathematics explorations. The following are some thoughts that we conveyed to them about convincing argument as a key feature of generalization.

Expectations

It is unrealistic to expect students' convincing arguments to look like those constructed by professional mathematicians, but at the same time, it is entirely fair to expect middle and high school students to produce the fundamental part of the convincing argument: a coherent string of thoughts that convinces fellow students of a mathematical result. Convincing arguments, even those produced by middle and high school students, must meet certain criteria:

- **Convincing arguments leave nothing to inference.** A solid convincing argument is clear about assumptions being made, is based on facts, and has no gaps or holes.

- **Convincing arguments are tied to the original context of the problem.** If students use tables, diagrams, equations, or other tools to describe a problem situation, their justification must link the representation to the original context. For example, valid convincing arguments for the following Towering Numbers questions must tie answers to the original context of the problem: the visual image of the tower.

- **Convincing arguments stand up to any challenge.** A good convincing argument includes a justification for each step.

These are, in effect, standards for convincing argument. Students should be aware of these standards and see exemplars of each. While the language and form of these arguments will differ from those of professional mathematicians, students should aspire to have these key elements in all of their convincing arguments.

To see how these criteria play out in actual student work, consider the following convincing arguments made by Linked Learning students on the Towering Numbers activity.

Suppose you wanted to build a tower with 25 rows using the same design. Describe how you could figure out how many bricks you would need for the twenty-fifth (longest) row.

I would make my tower. I know that the twenty-fifth block is the middle block, and that there is one less block on each side, which would make it 24 blocks on each side. If you multiply 24 by 2 and add the middle block, you get 49 blocks.

A very large tower was built using the same design. The longest row had 299 bricks in it. How many rows of bricks did the tower have? Tell how you figured out your answer.

150 rows. We knew that both sides added together equaled 299, that the middle number made it equal an odd number. So you take one off and have 298. Then, since you have *two* sides, you divided 298 by *2*, which equals 149 on each side; then you have to add one block for the one you took away and have 150.

While these students are clearly writing in middle and high school language and using their own format, their responses contain the key ingredients of a convincing argument: (1) They leave nothing to inference: The students lay out their thinking clearly, so that it is easy to follow their reasoning, and they include all of the important steps, so that there are no gaps in reasoning. (2) They are tied to the original context of the problem: The arguments are based on the visual image of the tower. (3) They stand up to any challenge: They provide a justification for each step they take to come up with their answers.

Suggestions for Cultivating Convincing Arguments

Fostering convincing-argument skills among students takes time and practice. It can, and should, be a part of regular instruction, with teachers asking students why their answers work, and getting students into the habit of writing down their arguments in a coherent way. Sometimes a convincing argument for a statement may be out of reach for students, in which case teachers can acknowledge that there exists a convincing argument for the statement even though the students cannot do it. Doing this will help to remove the mystery from mathematics and empha-

TABLE 5–1. *Questions to Help Develop Convincing Arguments*

Audience	Sample Questions: for students to ask themselves
In preparing to convince a friend or person who thinks like you, you want to ask yourself:	What do I know for sure? What do I think may be true? What do I want to be able to show? What did I do to convince myself that I covered all cases? Did I check for mistakes? What will be some key things to emphasize in my explanation?
In preparing to convince a group that may include skeptics, presentation may play a greater role. You may want to ask yourself some further questions:	What examples can best make my case? What will best communicate my argument: words? a picture? a table? an equation? . . . ? Am I prepared to have them test my rule on any case they select? What counterarguments should I anticipate?

size that mathematics is not an arcane collection of rules and formulas, but a field whose results are the product of logical reasoning applied to basic statements.

Questions will help students who are having trouble developing convincing arguments. Students might ask themselves questions such as the ones shown in Table 5–1.

Teachers, too, can be helpful. For example, for the Towering Numbers activity, the following questions, which could motivate convincing argument, were noted by Linked Learning classroom observers:

- One teacher asked this question of a small group: "What is true of every row?" This question seems, for this activity, a version of the more generic "What do you know for sure?" and seems to prod the students toward "And what do you think may be true?"

- Another teacher visited a small group and spotted "$2 \times 25 - 1$" on a student's paper. She asked the group: "Why does '$2 \times 25 - 1$' work?"

- Yet another teacher saw that one of her students had written down the number 49 as an answer to one of the questions. She asked the student, "Where does the 49 come from?"

- A fourth teacher saw the square root of 10,000 on a student's paper and said, "The square root of 10,000 tells me; it doesn't show me. You need to show me."

Other possibly helpful questions include the following:

- How did you get your answer?

- How can you be sure that your answer is right?

- Why is your formula right?

- Why did you do that?

- What are you trying to find out?

Example Activities

Here are some activities that can highlight the features of generalization we have discussed, in the context of functional relations: globalizing, extending, and making convincing arguments.

Paper Folding

This classic problem gives students an opportunity to find a rule, describe it in recursive and closed forms, and come up with a convincing argument for why the rule works.

Paper Folding

Using strips of paper, investigate the relationship between the number of times the strip is folded in half and the number of creases formed. How many creases will the paper strip have if it is folded in half *n* times? Does the direction of successive folds make a difference? Why does this pattern hold?

Each time the strip is folded in half, the number of sections of paper doubles and the number of creases is one less than this number. The picture shows the sections and creases after two folds. Moving from this recursive description to a more general, closed description, we can ask, "What steps am I doing over and over? How can I describe the steps without using specific inputs?" We might wonder what numbers fit into the sequence of creases and what numbers do not (a question of Doing–Undoing). For example, "If I keep folding, will exactly 56 creases appear at some stage?"

Expressing the relation in terms of input and output, we can say that after the paper has been folded n times, there are $2^n - 1$ creases. This problem lends itself to a convincing argument in answer to the question, "Why does this rule work?" Think about how many layers of paper there are at any point in the folding process.

Painted Cubes

This problem give students more practice in building rules. Visualizing skills come in handy in this problem as students try to understand why their rules work. It is especially advantageous, in light of our perspective on algebraic habits of mind, because it requires a decomposition, or undoing, of the cube.

Painted Cubes[4]

A cube with edges of length 2 centimeters is built from centimeter cubes. If you paint the faces of this cube and then break it into centimeter cubes, how many cubes will be painted on three faces? How many will be painted on two faces? on one face? How many will be unpainted? What if the edge has a length different from 2? What if the length of the large cube is 3 cm? 50 cm? n cm?

A basic fact that is relevant here: A cube made of centimeter cubes with n centimeters on a side, the cube is made up of n^3-centimeter cubes. A cube with edges of length n will have eight cubes painted on three faces—the eight corner cubes. The cubes on the edge between two faces that are not on the corners will have two faces painted. Each edge has $n - 2$ such cubes, and there are 12 such edges; so, there are $12 (n - 2)$ cubes with two faces painted. For the first cube asked about, where $n = 2$, this means there are 0 cubes with two faces painted. For $n = 3$, there are 12 cubes with two faces painted.

The remaining cubes on the outside will have just one face painted. On each face, there are $(n - 2)^2$ such cubes, and there are six faces; so, there are $6(n - 2)^2$ cubes with exactly one face painted. The remaining cubes with no faces painted—the ones inside—form a cube themselves with edge length $n - 2$, meaning that the number of cubes with no faces painted is equal to $(n - 2)^3$.

Any cube with a side of n centimeters has n^3 cubes in it. The analysis we just went through shows that the total number of cubes is also equal to $8 + 12(n - 2) + 6(n - 2)^2 + (n - 2)^3$. So, this visual decomposition of the painted cube has an added mathematical benefit, namely, to emphasize the meaning of equivalence of algebraic expressions: $n^3 = 8 + 12(n - 2) + 6(n - 2)^2 + (n - 2)^3$. (Guiding question: How does this expression behave like that one?)

Matchstick Rectangles

Based on the experience of teachers in our projects, this is another activity that can be used at all levels of the grades 6 through 10 range. Like the Painted Cubes activity, this problem is most approachable if students visually "chunk." To come up with a rule for finding the total number of matches in this activity's arrangement, students can group matches in a uniform way, count the number of matches in their groups, and sum up to get the total number of matches. The ability to chunk is a habit of mind that comes in handy in many areas of mathematics. (Guiding question: What steps am I doing over and over?)

Matchstick Rectangles[5]
The picture shows a rectangle made up of two rows of four columns and of squares outlined by matches. How many matches would be needed to make a rectangle with R rows and C columns?

There are different ways to do visual chunking for this activity, a fact that, as in the Painted Cubes problem, can lead to a greater appreciation of the meaning of equivalence of algebraic expressions. The matches can be divided into two categories: horizontal matches and vertical matches. For an $R \times C$ rectangle (in the picture, $R = 2$ and $C = 4$), there will always be $R + 1$ rows of horizontal matches. Each row contains C matches. Thus, there are $C(R + 1)$ horizontal matches. A similar process yields the number of vertical matches. Summing up the two gives the total number of matches in an $R \times C$ rectangle. Other ways of chunking are possible, too. Did you use a different way?

Triangles

This problem, at a more advanced level, gives students more experience building rules by chunking and also give students an opportunity to use the habit of mind Abstracting from Computation. Furthermore, it provides opportunities for students to link recursive and closed descriptions of patterns.

Triangles[6]

Consider this sequence of diagrams:

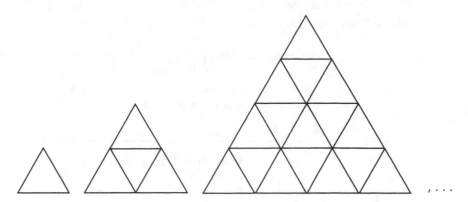

, . . .

The first diagram is made up of three line segments of equal length. You can think of the second diagram as made up of nine segments of that same length, and so on.

1. Find the number of segments of the given length that would be needed for the tenth diagram in this sequence.

2. Explain how you would find the number of segments of the given length that would be needed for the 100th diagram in this sequence.

3. How would you find the number of segments of the given length for any diagram in this sequence?

First, sketch the next diagram in the sequence and be aware of the rule you are using to sketch it. Was your rule based on previous steps? (Guiding question: How is the element in the sequence related to the ones that went before?) Or did you generate the diagram by the number of line segments in the base? Each represents a different kind of visual chunking of this problem. The former is a case of recursive thinking, while the latter is more a closed functional description. Chunking by the number of line segments in the base might go this way: At the nth stage, there are 2^{n-1} segments in the base. Counting vertically by level, there are $2^{n-1} - 1$, then $2^{n-1} - 2$, and so on, segments, for a total of $1 + 2 + 3 \ldots + 2^{n-1}$. You may recall from considering the Triangular Numbers problem $(1, 3, 6, 10, 15, \ldots)$ that the sum of 1 through m is $m(m + 1)/2$. So, with $m = 2^{n-1}$, we get $2^{n-2}(2^{n-1} + 1)$. The total number of segments comes by visually rotating the triangle to let the other two sides be the base, and so multiplying this number by 3. In the end, the nth triangle contains $3(2^{2n-3} + 2^{n-2})$ line segments.

Bee Genealogy

This problem deals with a popular number pattern that is familiar to many teachers and students. Exploring the number pattern gives students practice investigating recursive relationships.

Bee Genealogy[7]

Male bees hatch from unfertilized eggs and so have a mother but no father. Female bees hatch from fertilized eggs. How many ancestors does a male bee have in the twelfth generation back? How many of these are males? Generalize to any generation back.

After you investigate the first few generations above the original male, a familiar sequence appears—the Fibonacci Sequence: (1, 1, 2, 3, 5, 8, 13, . . .)—where each element is the sum of the previous two elements. Both the total number of bees and the number of males increase from one generation to the next in the same way as the Fibonacci Sequence. Why does the pattern hold? (Guiding question: How are things changing?)

Number Patterns

This problem gives students opportunities to practice globalizing. The pattern in this problem is hard to characterize at first glance, but after playing around with the structure of the number arrangements, many students in the grades 6 through 10 range can answer the questions about particular numbers and may be able to express a general rule, at least in words if not in symbols.

Number Patterns[8]

Below is an orderly way to arrange the whole numbers. What number is directly above 100? directly above 1000? What is a way to tell what number is directly above any given number?

```
 .
 .
 .
16  17  18  19  20  21
11  12  13  14  15
 7   8   9  10
 4   5   6
 2   3
 1
```

Because there are several things to attend to—visually and numerically—in this growth pattern, there are several answers to the questions, "How are things changing?" and "Is there information here that lets me predict what's going to happen?" Of particular interest is "What information might help me tell what number is directly above 100 or 1000?" To see what rows 100 and 1000 are in, one way is to figure out how to represent the last number in each row. The sequence $(1, 3, 6, 10, 15, \ldots)$ is familiar (the Triangular Numbers again), and the nth triangular number is $n(n + 1)/2$. Thus, the fifth number is $5 \times 6/2 = 15$. So, the nth row ends with the number $n(n + 1)/2$.

On the other end, what number begins the nth row? (This is an Undoing question, a variation of "Can I decompose this number or expression into helpful components?") A little observation indicates that the nth row begins with the number $[n(n + 1)/2] - n + 1$, which equals $(n^2 - n + 2)/2$. Furthermore, to get the number right above an element in the nth row, add n to it. The fourteenth row ends with $14 \times 15/2 = 105$, and it begins with $(14^2 - 14 + 2)/2 = 92$, so this is the row that 100 is in. The number right above it is, therefore, 114. Use similar reasoning to show that 1045 is above 1000. Generalize the rule you are using to figure the number right above any given number.

Arithmagons Extensions

This problem gives students a chance to *extend* the arithmagons problem from Chapter 4.

Arithmagons Extensions[9]
A secret number is assigned to each vertex of a quadrilateral. On each side of the quadrilateral is written the sum of the secret numbers at its ends. For example, secret numbers 3, 4, 9, and 16 produce

Do any other secret numbers produce the same quadrilateral? Find a rule for revealing the secret numbers.

When used as an extension of the triangle arithmagon, this activity elicits the following guiding question: How is this calculating situation like/unlike that one? To reveal one way the quadrilateral is unlike the triangle, try another number instead of 3 in the upper left corner. You should be able to find three other numbers that fit with your choice as a set of four secret numbers. What rule did you use? It is likely that your thinking through a rule included some Doing-Undoing, as in, "Can I decompose this number into helpful components?"

One way to think about it is to think of a general number a in the upper left corner. Then, going clockwise, you have $7 - a$, $13 - (7 - a) = a + 6$, and $25 - (a + 6) = 19 - a$. How is this different from the triangle? Why is it different? In the quadrilateral, what happens if you change one of the numbers on the sides (e.g., if you change 25 to 24)? You can extend to other shapes, as well.

Notes

1. This problem and the corresponding student work were taken, with permission, from a Linked Learning classroom.
2. Excerpted from *Problem-mathics* by C. Greenes, R. Spungin, and J. Dombrowski; copyright 1977 by C. Greenes, published by Creative Publications.
3. This teaching strategy was suggested by a Linked Learning teacher and facilitator, Joan Grampp.
4. From *Connected Mathematics Project, Frogs, Fleas, and Painted Cubes, Gr. 8* by Glenda Luppan, James Fey, William Fitzgerald, Susan Friel, and Elizabeth Phillips; copyright 1998 by Michigan State University, Glenda Lappan, James Fey, William Fitzgerald, Susan Friel, and Elizabeth Phillips. Reprinted by Dale Seymoor Publications.
5. This activity is from Mason, J. 1996. "Expressing Generality and Roots of Algebra." In *Approaches to Algebra: Perspectives for Research and Teaching,* eds. N. Bednarz, C. Kieran & L. Lee, 80. Dordrecht, The Netherlands: Kluwer, Academic Publishers. With kind permission from Kluwer Academic Publishers.
6. Excerpted from "The Overland Trail," *Interactive Mathematics Program Year 1,* copyright 1997 by Interactive Mathematics Program. Published by Key Curriculum Press (Emeryville, CA).
7. From *Thinking Mathematically*, by John Mason; copyright 1982 by Addison-Wesley Publishing Company. Reprinted by permission.
8. This activity is from Page, D. *University of Illinois Arithmetic Project: Maneuvers on Lattices.* In *MathFINDER CD-ROM.* Armonk, NY: The Learning Team.
9. This activity is adapted from Mason, J. 1985. *Thinking Mathematically,* 160. Wokingham, England: Addison Wesley.

References and Further Reading

Bell, A. 1995. "Purpose in School Algebra." *The Journal of Mathematical Behavior* 14 (1): 41–75.

Brown, S. & M. Walter. 1983. *The Art of Problem Solving.* Philadelphia: Franklin Press.

Friedlander, A. & R. Hershkowitz. 1997. "Reasoning with Algebra." *Mathematics Teacher* 90 (6): 442–47.

Harel, G. & D. Tall. 1991. "The General, the Abstract, and the Generic in Advanced Mathematics." *For the Learning of Mathematics* 11 (1): 38–42.

Langrall, C.W. & J.O. Swafford. 1997. "Grade Six Students' Use of Equations to Describe and Represent Problem Situations." Paper presented at the annual meeting of the American Educational Research Association, Chicago, Illinois, March 1997.

Lee, L. 1996. "An Initiation into Algebraic Culture Through Generalization Activities." In *Approaches to Algebra: Perspectives for Research and Teaching,* eds. N. Bednarz, C. Kieran & L. Lee, 87–106. Dordrecht, The Netherlands: Kluwer Academic Publishers.

Lee, L. & D. Wheeler. 1987. *Algebraic Thinking in High School Students: Their Conceptions of Generalization and Justification* (research report). Montreal: Concordia University, Department of Mathematics.

Mason, J. 1996. "Expressing Generality and Roots of Algebra." In *Approaches to Algebra: Perspectives for Research and Teaching,* eds. N. Bednarz, C. Kieran & L. Lee, 65–86. Dordrecht, The Netherlands: Kluwer Academic Publishers.

Schwartz, J. & M. Yerushalmy. 1992. "Getting Students to Function in and with Algebra." In *The Concept of Function: Aspects of Epistemology and Pedagogy* (MAA Notes, Vol. 25), eds. G. Harel & E. Dubinsky, 261–89. Washington, D.C.: Mathematical Association of America.

6

Fostering Symbol Sense

Algebra and Symbolic Expression

As a subject, algebra defies any concise definition, largely because it has so many facets and uses. However, there is one thing that distinguishes it, even in the minds of those outside the education community: the use and manipulation of letter symbols. This impression is widespread for good reasons. Wheeler (1996) suggests that one of the "big ideas" related to algebra is "the idea, or the awareness, that an as-yet-unknown number, that a general number, and that a variable can each be symbolized and operated on 'as if' it was a number" (322).

There is a risk in the popularity of this impression about the role of symbolism in algebra, especially among teachers: that algebra and algebraic thinking become equated with the use of letter symbols. When this happens, use of letter symbols ceases to be a means to an end and becomes only an end, in and of itself; instead of using letter symbols to engage in higher order thinking such as generalizing and abstracting, people manipulate symbols as an end, in and of itself. We were reminded, during a session with a group of middle school teacher leaders involved in one of our projects, of the deep-seated mindsets of many teachers about the value of symbol manipulation. During this session, groups of teachers were working on Sums of Consecutive Numbers, the activity discussed in Chapters 2 and 4.

Sums of Consecutive Numbers

$$3 + 4 = 7$$

$$2 + 3 + 4 = 9$$

$$4 + 5 + 6 + 7 = 22$$

These problems are examples of sums of consecutive numbers. The number 7 is shown as the sum of two consecutive numbers. The number 9 is shown as the sum of three consecutive numbers. The number 22 is shown as the sum of four consecutive numbers. In this activity, you will explore what numbers can and cannot be made by sums of consecutive numbers.

The teachers had explored the mathematics in pairs and had been asked to think about where they had found themselves generalizing from calculation patterns they saw. Each pair reported back to the full group, using the overhead projector.

Doris, who taught in elementary school before joining the leadership team, reported on an investigation into numbers that can be represented as sums of four consecutive whole numbers:

"First we wrote them down in sequence:

1. $10 = 1 + 2 + 3 + 4$

2. $14 = 2 + 3 + 4 + 5$

3. $18 = 3 + 4 + 5 + 6$

4. $22 = 4 + 5 + 6 + 7$

    .

    .

    .

Then I looked at the right side of the equation signs and tried to capture what the pattern was in the computations. I noticed that you get the number on the left-hand side by taking the number of the equation, say, the ath equation, which is also the first number in the string of four on the right side. Add a to $a + 3$, the last number in the string, and multiply all times 2."

Doris then wrote "$2[a + (a + 3)]$" on the overhead and continued, "So, if you are in equation number 1, take $1 + (1 + 3)$, or 5 and multiply times 2 to get 10. In equation 2, $2 + (2 + 3)$, or 7, times 2 is 14, and so on." After brief acknowledgment that the formula worked, the group moved on.

As others talked about their investigations, someone used the algebraic expression $5n + 15$ to describe the numbers that can be represented as the sum of five consecutive whole numbers. Doris grimaced slightly but noticeably and, as soon as she had a chance to say something, came to the overhead projector and pointed to her expression, $2[a + (a + 3)]$. She said: "This is just simply $4a + 6$. That would be a simpler way to write it. I didn't need to write it out the long way." With that, she sat down, looking somewhat embarrassed.

Later, the facilitator realized that Doris' original expression, $2[a + (a + 3)]$, not only gave a clear rule for producing the sequence of numbers that can be written as the sum of four consecutive whole numbers, but also had embedded in it another generalization about numbers: that in any string of four consecutive integers, the sum of the first and last equals the sum of the middle two. In terms of giving insight into where Doris was generalizing from calculation patterns she saw, the topic of the group's discussion, this was an expression *preferable* to $4a + 6$.

There is a lesson here about the value of comparing and analyzing equivalent expressions, a point we return to later in this chapter. However, there also is a lesson here about the deep-seated mindsets regarding what has value in algebra—in this case, the most succinct symbolic representation. Doris' embarrassment was apparently rooted in a belief in the value of simplified expressions. However, in this instance, her original expression brought out her thinking and the underlying mathematics in a meaningful way, which would not have been possible had she simplified her expression.

Of course, there is great value in the succinctness and standardization of symbolic expression in algebra, and it is important that all students learn to use algebraic symbolism to express and communicate generalization, to reveal algebraic structure, to establish connections, and to formulate mathematical arguments. However, it is important to achieve these goals without pushing students prematurely and inappropriately toward using symbolic expression. Instead, it is important to build toward appropriate use of symbols by valuing the productive kinds of algebraic thinking that do not require symbolic expression.

Ideally, just as we want to foster, from the early grades, students' development of algebraic-thinking habits of mind, such as Building Rules to Represent Functions, Doing–Undoing, and Abstracting from Computation, we want them to develop good "symbol sense." In this chapter, we examine obstacles to learning how to understand and work with symbols, aspects of symbol sense that are important to heed, and implications for how to foster the development of symbol sense. We conclude with a sampling of activities that we feel can help spur the development of symbol sense.

Obstacles to Symbol Sense

Understanding the meaning of symbols and having a facility with symbols is difficult not only for algebra students, but also for many adults. We were reminded of the difficulties imposed by symbols one day during a summer institute for one of our projects.

On this day, we were concentrating on the mathematical habit of mind we call Doing–Undoing, the capacity to both build and take apart processes, or to investigate a process or relation by starting at the end and working backward (see Chapter 1). In this context, the teachers had been working in small groups on an activity, the beginning of which appears after this paragraph. In effect, the activity asks one to start with a division remainder and undo the process of division to arrive at starting conditions. The Age problem, which appeared in Chapter 2, is another version of this problem.

1. Characterize the numbers for which you get a remainder of 1 when you divide by 5.

2. Characterize the numbers for which you get a remainder of 1 when you divide by 5, and a remainder of 2 when you divide by 3.

One of the small groups included Charles and Rhonda, both of whom were new to middle school and to the pressures of preparing middle school students to become proficient in algebra. For the second part of the problem, they wrote a string of numbers surrounded by numerous computations: 11, 26, 41, 56, 71, ... "We think this is all of them," said Charles. "But now what do we do with them?" asked Rhonda. The facilitator said, "Tell me what you see in that string of numbers," and, almost together, they said, "You start with 11 and go up by 15 each time." "But," Rhonda said, with some agitation, "there's gotta be more." Curious as to whether they saw any significance in the constant difference of 15, the facilitator asked, and learned that they had cranked out the first five numbers through computation and then had noticed the constant difference of 15.

Later, representatives from different groups came to the overhead projector to display what they had done and, in particular, to reveal which lines of their thinking "undid" the division process. During one of these presentations, a teacher was filling the transparency with a variety of references to what his group had done. In the course of this, he wrote $11 + 15n$ and said almost offhandedly that "this represents all the numbers that leave a remainder of 2 when divided by 3, and a remainder of 1 when divided by 5." From her seat, Rhonda said enthusiastically, "That's it! That's what we need to learn how to do." Presumably, Rhonda's "that" referred to forming an algebraic expression describing an infinite set of numbers—in this case, the arithmetic progression starting with 11 and progressing by constant differences of 15. Those who have been immersed in algebraic thinking for a long time can forget what a sizable leap it is to go from generating a finite string of numbers that are the same distance apart to having the symbol sense to form the concise symbolic expression that captures those numbers and all like them.

Rhonda and Charles' struggle is representative of difficulties many people have when using letter symbols. Working with letter symbols is challenging, in part, because of a set of fundamental obstacles that can get in the way of understanding the very *concept* of symbolic expression. Included in such obstacles are the following:

- **Differences between natural language and algebraic expression**: Tall and Thomas (1991) summarize this obstacle: "There is considerable cognitive conflict between the deeply ingrained implicit understanding of natural language and the symbolism of algebra" (125). One example offered is the expression $2 + 3x$, which is read left to right, but processed right to left, since the 3 and the x are multiplied before adding 2. Similarly, newcomers to algebraic expression can read the expression ab as a and b and so equate it with the expression $a + b$. These are two of the many ways in which the differences between natural language and algebraic expression can confound those who are trying to learn algebra.

- **Multiple meanings attached to letter symbols**: Letters in algebraic statements can refer to a single unknown number, as in $8n - 7 = 33$, but they also can refer to general numbers, as in the expression $8n - 7$, or to varying quantities, as in the function $n \rightarrow 8n - 7$. In prealgebra years, students often see elementary examples of letters that represent unknowns. It is often a challenge to interpret a switch in meaning. Even more complicated are statements in which the meaning is mixed. For example, textbooks often describe the general linear relationship by the formula $y = mx + b$. Here the y and x represent variables and the m and b represent "parameters." Arcavi (1994) points out that "the kinds of mathematical objects one obtains by substituting in them are very different" (30). In terms of the Cartesian plane, choosing numerical values for x and y fixes a point in the plane [the point $(x, mx + b)$]; choosing numerical values for m and b fixes a line in the plane [all the points (x,y) satisfying $y = mx + b$].

- **Cognitive difficulty in translating to algebraic expressions**: One of the central purposes of algebra is to model real situations mathematically, and a key to this is the capacity to translate from natural language to algebraic expression. This is the core challenge, for example, in algebra word problems. However, while some situations translate quite naturally (e.g., statements of equality, such as, "Express symbolically the relationship 'y is equal to the sum of x and 10'") others do not (e.g., statements comparing unequal quantities, such as, "Express symbolically the relationship 'y is 10 more than x'") (MacGregor & Stacey 1993). Algebraically, they are equivalent statements. Cognitively, however, they call for different mental representations.

MacGregor and Stacey asked a group of several hundred ninth-graders to do the following tasks, each of which involves a comparison of unequal quantities:

1. "The number y is eight times the number z." Write this information in mathematical symbols.

2. "s and t are numbers. s is eight more than t." Write an equation showing the relation between s and t.

3. "The Niger river in Africa is y meters long. The Rhine in Europe is z meters long. The Niger is three times as long as the Rhine." Write an equation that shows how y is related to z.

For each of these three tasks, fewer than a third of the students were able to write a correct algebraic statement. Significantly, for each of the tasks, about half of the students wrote reversed equations such as $8y = z$ for the first one and $t = s + 8$ for the second. By contrast, the students did fine with this problem:

"z is equal to the sum of 3 and y." Write this information in mathematical symbols.

Therefore, it appears they were not misreading the statements of comparison of unequal quantities. Rather, the difficulty seems to be at the cognitive level. The authors state, "Students should be made aware that some relationships (such as 'eight more than') are easy to express in natural language and easy to comprehend but must be paraphrased, reorganized, or reinterpreted before they can be expressed mathematically" (229).

Facets of Symbol Sense

The kind of symbol sense that we recommend all students develop to support their algebraic thinking has several components (adapted from Arcavi 1994, Fey 1990), including those on the following list. This is not intended to be a comprehensive listing of what constitutes good symbol sense for algebra learners. However, the aspects of symbol sense listed serve as a helpful framework for this chapter for two reasons: (1) They address the heart of the teacher concerns that led to the writing of this chapter, and (2) they are closely related to the three algebraic-thinking habits of mind featured in this book: Doing–Undoing, Building Rules to Represent Functions, and Abstracting from Computation.

Knowing When to Call on Symbols and When Not To

Related algebraic-thinking guiding questions:

- How can I describe the steps without using specific inputs?
- Does my rule work for all cases?

It often makes sense to call on symbols when asked to show that some statement about numbers is "always true," as in, "What is always true about the difference between a whole number and its square?" ("Let's see. If n is the whole number, then $n^2 - n$ is the same as $n(n - 1)$, so one thing I can say is that the difference is the product of two consecutive numbers . . . .")

Sometimes the rush to "algebraicize" can make things more complicated mathematically than they need to be. Mason (1996) writes about how a group of students dealt with the following problem:

A number of eggs were brought to market. The number left remainders of 1, 2, 3, 4, 5, and 0 when put in groups of 2, 3, 4, 5, 6, and 7, respectively. What is the least number of eggs brought to market?

Mason observes, "The students rushed in to write down equations involving unknowns. . . . However, they were unable to do anything with their equations. This is an algorithm-seeking question, not a simple algebra question" (75).

Being Able to Interpret the Meaning of Symbols

In the previous section, we mentioned the multiple meanings that symbols can have in algebraic representation. For example, in $y = mx + b$, the description of the general linear relationship, the letters x and y have a different meaning than the letters m and b. Sometimes, even when only one letter occurs in an algebraic expression, it is important to look behind the symbol to interpret meaning. For example, in Chapter 5 we talked about the difficulty students can have in justifying a generalization such as, "The sum of two consecutive whole numbers is odd." In one study, many students were able to represent consecutive whole numbers with n and $n + 1$, and they were even able to express the sum as $2n + 1$; however, they were not able to see through the symbols in $2n + 1$ to conclude, "This has to be an odd number because $2n$ is a multiple of 2 and is always going to be even."

Related algebraic-thinking guiding questions:

- Is there information here that lets me predict what's going to happen?

- Now that I have an equation, how do the numbers (parameters) in the equation relate to the problem context?

Being Able to Inspect an Algebraic Operation and Predict the Form of the Result

An example of this aspect of symbol sense is knowing ahead of time that multiplying the expressions $(x + 6)$ and $(x^2 + 4)$ will result in an expression involving x^3 as the highest power of x. A more advanced example is seeing without computing that most terms will drop out if $(y - 1)$ is multiplied by $(1 + y + y^2 + \ldots + y^n)$.

Related algebraic-thinking guiding questions:

- How can I predict what's going to happen without doing all the calculation?

- What are my operation shortcuts for getting from here to there?

Knowing How to Scan an Expression or Formula and Make Rough Estimates of the Patterns That Would Emerge in Numeric or Graphical Representations

For example, you may recognize that if $4n + 5$ is represented on a graph for all natural numbers n, the points will all lie on a straight line.

Related algebraic-thinking guiding questions:

- How does this expression behave like that one?

- What are other ways to write this expression that will bring out hidden meaning?

- How can I write this expression in terms of things I care about?
- How are things changing?

Knowing How to Scan a Table or Graph, or to Interpret Verbally Stated Conditions to Identify the Likely Form of the Symbolic Expression of the Associated Algebraic Rule

This facet of symbol sense is, in essence, the reverse of the previous one. An example is recognizing (1) that if successive differences in a table of function values for inputs 1, 2, 3, . . . increase as an arithmetic progression, then the rule will include some constant times x^2; and (2) that this will be the highest power of x in the rule's formula. For example:

Input	Function Values	Successive Differences
1	5	
2	8	3
3	13	5
4	20	7
5	29	9
.	.	.

Related algebraic-thinking guiding questions:

- Is there information here that lets me predict what's going to happen?
- How are things changing?

Recommendations for Ongoing Attention to Symbol Sense

There are many ways in which teachers can support the development of symbol sense in their students on an everyday basis. They can start by both being aware of obstacles students face as they work with symbols and encouraging the development of various facets of symbol sense in their students. Following are some specific recommendations for developing symbol sense in students.

Use Visual Representation

To help smooth the transition to using letter symbols, give students plenty of opportunities to work with visual symbols that are not letter symbols. Often it is more natural to represent a quantity with a picture rather than a letter symbol. For example, when comparing prices of a cap and an umbrella, it can make more sense to represent the price of the cap with a picture of a cap and the price of an umbrella with a picture of an umbrella rather than to represent the prices with letter symbols. To help students make the transition to using letter symbols, it can help to first use pictorial symbols to represent quantities before moving on to the use of letter symbols. Finding Prices, an activity in the Example Activities section, requires that students represent prices of objects with pictures of objects. Chickens, another activity in the Example Activities section, also invites the use of pictorial symbols.

Capitalize on Opportunities

While it is important to be cautious about rushing students into using symbolic representation, it is equally important to look for opportunities to guide students toward using symbolic expression when their work shows signs of their being ready. For example, sometimes students will generate a handful of numerical examples that seem to reveal a consistent underlying process, which, in turn, lends itself to a smooth transition to symbolic expression.

Consider Figure 6–1, an example on the Sums of Consecutive Numbers activity. (This example is also discussed in Chapter 7, in another context.) Although the student falls well below standards for "describing the shortcuts" and "telling how," it is easy to infer that there is a well-reasoned procedure underlying the disconnected computations, one that seems based on and works backward from the recognition that three consecutive numbers beginning with n have the sum $3n + 3$; four consecutive numbers have the sum $4n + 6$; five have the sum $5n + 10$; and so on. This inference invites instructional questions such as, "Suppose you were given a number n that is divisible by 3. Could you express it as a sum of three consecutive numbers?"

FIGURE 6–1.   *Student Work on Sums of Consecutive Numbers Activity*

4. Use the discoveries you made in question #2 to come up with shortcuts for writing the following numbers as the sum of two or more consecutive numbers. Describe the shortcuts you created and tell how you used them to write each of the numbers below as sums of consecutive numbers.

a) 45   b) 57   c) 62   d) 75   e) 80

$$\frac{45-1}{2} = \frac{44}{2} \neq 2$$

$$22 + 22$$

$$\frac{45-15}{6} = \frac{30}{6} = 5$$

$$\frac{45-3}{3} = \frac{42}{3} = 14$$

$$5 + 6 + 7 + 8 + 9 + 10$$

$$14 + 15 + 6$$

$$\frac{45-10}{5} = \frac{35}{5} = 7$$

$$7 + 8 + 9 + 10 + 11$$

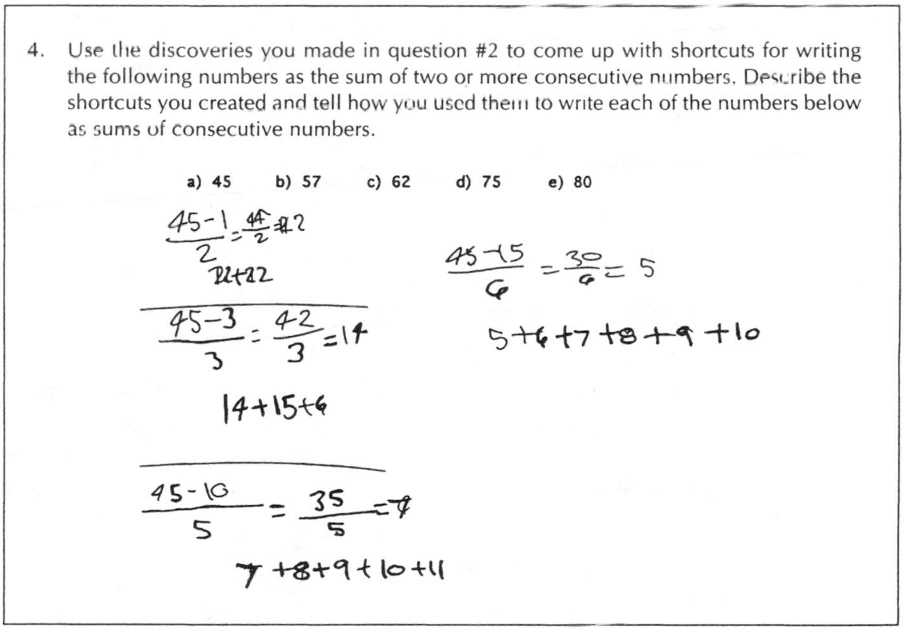

Opportunities for guiding students toward symbolic expression arose in another class, which was working on a version of the Postage Stamp problem (discussed in Chapter 2).

Three- and Four-Cent Postage Stamps

The post office has only 3-cent and 4-cent stamps. They would like to make a table showing postage amounts for different combinations of stamps. They have started the table below. Finish filling in the table.

Postage Amounts for Different Combinations of 3¢ and 4¢ Stamps

Number of 3¢ stamps

	0	1	2	3	4	5	6	7
0	0	3	6					
1	4	7	10					
2	8	11	14					
3								
4								
5								
6								
7								

Number of 4¢ stamps

The class filled in the table, which extends as far as 49 cents. The teacher then led a discussion about finding combinations of 3-cent and 4-cent stamps worth more than 49 cents. The following was taken from the notes of another teacher who observed the class:

Teacher Questions/Comments	Student Reactions
The largest number in the table is 49. Is it possible to buy 3-cent and 4-cent stamps worth 50 cents? How many of each would you buy?	Lawrence: "Add one more 4 and one less 3 to 49 to get 50."
	Roberto: "51 cents is possible, too."
How did you do that, Roberto, without the table?	Roberto: "You keep adding on 4 cents and taking away 3 cents. You can keep on going."

The last question asked by the teacher is a variation on these algebraic-thinking guiding questions:

- How can I predict what's going to happen without doing all of the calculations?
- What are my operation shortcuts for getting from here to there?

Though no use of symbolic expression occurred in this interaction, the teacher could have gone on to ask questions to develop students' symbol sense, had she thought it appropriate at the time. She could have pushed Roberto to express his rule with symbols by asking questions such as the following one: "If I gave you any number *n* and wanted to buy a combination of 3-cent and 4-cent stamps, the total worth of which is *n* cents, how would you figure out how many 3-cent and 4-cent stamps I would need to buy?"

Engage Students in Bridging Activities

In the preceding Sums of Consecutive Numbers example, we imagined the teacher asking a question that helped the student bridge from the set of numerical examples to a general number *n*. There are activities that have this bridging potential built into them. For example, Demana and Leitzel (1988) (see also Kieran & Chalouh 1993) posed the following problem to prealgebra students.

For some rectangles, the length of the rectangle is 4 centimeters more than the width. Complete the following table:

Width (cm)	Length (cm)	Perimeter (cm)	Area (cm²)
1			
5			
8.4			
12			
w			

Algebraic-thinking guiding questions that teachers and students could ask to help students with the general case:

- What steps am I doing over and over?
- How can I describe the steps without using specific inputs?
- When I do the same thing with different numbers, what still holds true? What changes?
- Now that I have an equation, how do the numbers (parameters) in the equation relate to the problem context?

After the students completed the table, Demana and Leitzel asked them questions related to the table that helped them bridge the use of symbols as unknowns via the use of symbols as variables, such as, "If $w^2 + 4w = 45$, what is w?"

Width (cm)	Length (cm)	Perimeter (cm)	Area (cm²)
1	5	12	5
5	9	28	45
8.4	12.4	41.6	104.16
12	16	56	192
w	$w + 4$	$4w + 8$	$w^2 + 4w$

Exploit Equivalent Expressions

This chapter opened with a story about a teacher rejecting an algebraic expression she had constructed, in favor of a simpler equivalent expression. In that case, an opportunity was missed to analyze the advantages each expression offered for understanding the mathematics more deeply. In the course of modeling problem situations, students often develop different but equivalent expressions. By exploiting these occurrences as opportunities to compare and analyze for meaning, teachers can foster symbol sense. Arcavi (1994) writes about the variety of interactions that can be built around students' development of equivalent expressions for the following problem (33).

In this following arrangement of n tables, x indicates a seat for a single person, and "..." indicates a variable number of tables. How many people can be seated?

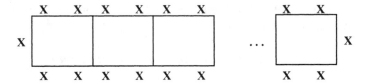

Arcavi writes, "One possible way of solving the problem is to regard it as a perimeter problem; thus, the number of seats will be $2(2n) + 1 + 1$, namely $4n + 2$. Another way is to count the number of seats at the tables which can seat only 4, namely, $n - 2$, and then add 10 more seats for the extremes, giving $4(n - 2) + 10$.

One can pose the reverse question: Which way did one count if, for example, the resulting expression was $5n - (n - 2)$?" The point of this kind of questioning is to sharpen students' symbol sense, in particular, around the meanings attached to equivalent expressions. For more examples of this kind, see the Tiling Garden Beds and Towering Numbers problems in the Example Activities section of this chapter, the Triangles and Matchstick Rectangles problems in the Example Activities section of Chapter 5, and the Toothpick Squares problem in the body of Chapter 5.

Look for Opportunities to Have Students Relate Expressions and Equations to the Original Context of the Problem

One of the teachers in our projects did this nicely when her students were working on the following problem:

Look at the table below. It is a table that describes tree growth in inches per month:

Months	0	1	2	3	4	5	6	...	10		n
Inches		1	4	7	10	13			28		

1. Write an equation that describes the growth of the tree from month to month.

2. Using the equation written in question 1, explain why, in the first month, the tree only grows to 1 inch.

3. What is the value of the height in inches at month 0? What is this value's meaning?[1]

As the teacher was doing this activity, she was observed by another project teacher. The observer recorded variations of the following interactions in several small groups. In each group, the students had filled in the table with more data and were attempting to construct a formula out of the data.

Teacher Questions	Student Responses
So, what is happening in the table?	"It goes down 2" [Writes "$3n - 2$."]
So, if it is $3n - 2$, what does the -2 mean?	"The seed is 2 inches below the ground."

The last question asked by the teacher is a variation on this algebraic-thinking guiding question:

- Now that I have an equation, how do the numbers (parameters) in the equation relate to the problem context?

To the teacher, it was important that the students relate parts of the equation back to the context of the problem—in this case, the constant -2 in the formula. By asking students to describe the meaning of the terms in the formula, we believe the teacher increases the chances that students will develop symbol sense. For examples of problems that invite reflection about the relationship between expressions and problem contexts, see the Tiling Garden Beds and Towering Numbers problems in the Example Activities section of this chapter.

Ask Students to Undo Processes Involving Symbols

We mentioned earlier that symbol sense involves being able to inspect algebraic computations and to predict the form of the results. One way to foster this capacity is to challenge students to undo as well as do computational processes. For example, in the problem, Multiplication of Binomials, in the Example Activities section of this chapter, students undo the process of multiplying polynomials. Undoing processes of algebraic representation also can provide good practice. For example, when students work on graphing polynomials on the coordinate plane, have them undo the process: Give them the graph of a polynomial and ask them questions about the form of the polynomial. Similar questions can be asked when moving between symbolic representations and other nongraphical representations, such as tables and diagrams. Chapter 7 looks in more depth at linking multiple representations in these ways.

Take Advantage of Technology

Historically, the use of letters to symbolize unknowns developed before the use of letters as variables, and this is the order in which they have been introduced in schools. Computers and graphing calculators have made it possible for students to have earlier experiences with letters as variables, by making it convenient to generate data for tables to model situations like this one: "Karen works part-time after school selling magazine subscriptions. She receives $20 as a base salary per week, plus $4 for each subscription she sells" (Kieran, Boileau & Garancon 1996, 280). There is research evidence of a lessening of some of the cognitive difficulties that students encounter in moving from letter-as-unknown to letter-as-variable, when this earlier, technology-based approach is employed, with students showing greater flexibility in switching back and forth between the two. "This flexibility was apparent, both in the action of some students' turning aside from their variable-based programs to their undoing methods when asked to actually solve certain types of problems, as well as in others' use of their functional representations to solve problem questions by means of a search for, say, a specific input value corresponding to the given output value of a problem question" (Kieran, Boileau & Garancon 1996, 275).

The full story about effects of computers and graphing calculators on students' development of symbol sense is not complete, but this evidence of increased flexibility in managing the meaning of letter symbols is promising.

Example Activities

The following activities can help to spur the development of symbol sense in students. They range from activities that can be used before students are fully comfortable with symbols (to help ease the transition to symbol use) to activities that can be used to enhance the symbol sense of students with a clear understanding of the meaning of symbols.

Finding Prices

Early experiences with pictorial representations of quantities can help smooth the transition to the use of letter symbols. Even better are problems like this one, which asks students to use reasoning they will use later on in algebra. While relying on pictorial representations, this problem foreshadows solving systems of two linear equations.

Finding Prices[2]
The following picture shows the costs of two combinations of umbrellas and hats:

1. Without calculating the price of each, determine whether the cap or the umbrella is more expensive. What is the difference in price between the cap and the umbrella?

2. Use the two pictures above to make a new combination of umbrellas and caps. Write down the cost of the combination.

3. Make a group of only caps or only umbrellas. Then find its price.

4. What is the price of one umbrella? one cap?

Associated guiding questions:

- Is there a rule or relationship here?
- How are things changing?

Many adults approach this problem by setting up a system of linear equations and solving for unknowns. However, students who have not yet taken algebra or who are new to algebra are often more flexible in their thinking and come up with creative ways to approach the problem. Many imagine taking away one umbrella and one cap from each grouping. That leaves an umbrella in the first group and a cap in the second group. How can this help you figure out whether the umbrella or the cap is more expensive and by how much? Questions that might help include the following: How is the price of each grouping affected when you take away a cap and an umbrella? What is different about the price of the new groupings, and what stays the same?

There are several ways to make combinations of umbrellas and caps and create groups of only caps or only umbrellas. Once you have created a group of only caps or only umbrellas, finding the price of one umbrella and one cap becomes much easier. You should eventually find that each umbrella is $28 and each cap is $24.

The steps your students take to solve this problem are equivalent to the steps they will take later on when they solve systems of equations: Instead of making combinations of umbrellas and caps, they will make combinations of variables, such as x and y; instead of making a group of only caps or only umbrellas, they will make a group of only x's or only y's.

Chickens

Although this problem does not dictate the use of pictorial representations in place of letter symbols, it does invite use of pictorial symbols and thus can be done by students who are not yet comfortable with letter symbols. Like the Finding Prices problem, this problem foreshadows work students will do later on in algebra when solving systems of equations; in essence, this problem asks students to solve a system of three equations with three unknowns.

Chickens[3]

Three chickens were weighed in pairs; the first pair weighed in at 10.6 kg, the second pair weighed 8.5 kg, and the third pair weighed 6.1 kg. How much would the scale read if all three chickens were weighed at the same time? How many kilograms does each chicken weigh?

There are many ways to do this problem. You could do it in a formal way by setting up three equations with three unknowns, solving for each unknown, and summing up to get the total weight of all three chickens. Alternatively, think about how many times each chicken has been weighed after the three weighings. Because each chicken is in exactly two of the three pairs that were weighed, each chicken was weighed exactly twice. Use this information along with the weights of the pairs to find a shortcut to find the sum of the weights of the three chickens. Once you know the sum of the weights, compare this sum with each equation to find the weight of individual chickens. Your answers should be as follows: The sum of the weights of the three chickens is 12.6 kg. The chickens' individual weights are 2 kg, 4.1 kg, and 6.5 kg.

As students work on this problem, they too may approach it in different ways; they may use actual letter symbols, they may draw pictures of chickens to represent the weights, or they may describe their solutions in words.

Multiplication of Binomials

Problems like this one can help develop symbol sense by requiring the undoing of a familiar process involving symbols.

Multiplication of Binomials

Find a binomial that multiplies by $4x - 3$ to give $16x^2 - 9$.

Associated guiding questions:

- What process reverses the one I'm using?
- Can I decompose this number or expression into helpful components?
- How does this expression behave like that one?

This problem can be solved by using the division algorithm to divide $4x - 3$ into $16x^2 - 9$, but such a process could become laborious. The problem could also be approached using a guess-and-check approach; in fact, such an approach is not dissimilar to the way many students learn to factor polynomials. While both of these methods are valid and will produce, eventually, a correct answer, there is a third method that people with strong symbol sense can employ that capitalizes on the relationship between the difference of squares: $a^2 - b^2 = (a - b)(a + b)$. Once you are able to recognize that this quadratic is a difference of two squares of the form $a^2 - b^2$ and the binomial given is of the form $a - b$, you can immediately conclude that the binomial that multiplies by $4x - 3$ is the binomial of the form $a + b$: $4x + 3$.

Rectangle Dimensions

This problem creates the demand for and shows the value of using symbols to solve problems.

Rectangle Dimensions[4]

Consider any rectangle. What would happen to its area if one of its dimensions were increased by 10% and the other decreased by 10%?

Associated guiding questions:

- How are things changing?
- How can I write the expression in terms of things I care about?

If x is the length and y is the width of the original rectangle, and the length x is increased by 10% while the width y is decreased 10%, then the new dimensions of the rectangle are $1.1x$ and $0.9y$. Thus, the new rectangle will have an area of $(1.1x)(0.9y) = 0.99xy$ and will be 99% of the old rectangle; its area will have decreased by 1%.

What about the case where the length x is decreased by 10% while the width y is increased by 10%? Can you find a way to think of it so you don't have to do all the calculation?

As an extension, you and your students can explore other amounts of increase and decrease and come up with a general rule showing what happens to area when dimensions are increased or decreased by any percentage, say, $m\%$ for some positive number m. How do you calculate $m\%$ of x? of y? What do you do next?

Magic Squares

This problem helps to develop symbol sense by requiring decisions as to when it is appropriate to invoke the use of symbols and also understand the meaning of a symbolic solution.

Magic Squares[5]

A magic square is one containing an array of numbers arranged in a square so that the sums of the numbers in each column, the sums of the numbers in each row, and the sums of the numbers on both diagonals are equal to the same number. In this problem you will examine 3×3 magic squares—squares with three numbers in each row and column. In the magic squares you examine, numbers can appear in the magic square more than once, and numbers can be positive, zero, or negative.

1. If possible, complete the empty squares to obtain magic squares with the stated sums. If it is impossible to do this, explain how you know it is impossible.

Sum of 9

	3	
2		1

Sum of 6

	2	
1		5

Sum of 8

	4	
2		2

2. In the problems above, you were given the sum of the columns, rows, and di-
    agonals of a magic square along with three numbers in a magic square: the
    number in the middle of the magic square, the number in the lower left cor-
    ner, and the number in the lower right corner. Sometimes you can create a
    magic square with the given numbers, and other times you can't. For what
    numbers is it possible to create a magic square, and for what numbers is it
    impossible?

Associated guiding questions:

- Is there a rule or relationship here?
- Why does the rule work the way it does?
- What steps am I doing over and over again?

The numbers in the first two magic squares can be found fairly easily with
straightforward computations:

1.

5	0	4
2	3	4
2	6	1

2.

-1	4	3
6	2	-2
1	0	5

It is impossible to create a magic square with the numbers in the part above, Sum
of 8. Why?

To figure out the answer to problem 2, you can use symbols to represent the
numbers that are given to you. Let S be the sum of the rows, columns, and diagonals of the magic square, and let x, y, and z be the three numbers in the magic
square, arranged like this:

Now fill in the empty boxes, using the same methods you used when working on the first two magic squares. For each empty box, you should be able to write an expression involving only the variables x, y, z, and S. Questions that can help include the following: What is the sum of the three numbers in the bottom row? How can you use that to figure out the middle number in the bottom row? How can you use the same strategy to find the other missing numbers?

Once you have completed filling in the empty boxes, do what you did when finding numbers for magic squares with specific numbers: Check that each row, column, and diagonal sum to S. As you do this, you will find some constraints on how x, y, z, and S are related to one another. You should eventually find that it is possible to create a magic square with x, y, z, and S as defined previously if and only if $S = 3y$. For a fuller discussion of this problem, see Arcavi (1994, 25).

Tiling Garden Beds

Tiling Garden Beds helps students develop their symbol sense by having them come up with and compare equivalent expressions describing a particular situation.

Tiling Garden Beds[6]

Here are three sizes of gardens framed with a single row of tiles. The white squares represent the tiles, and the dark squares represent the garden:

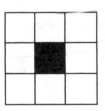
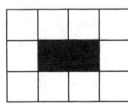
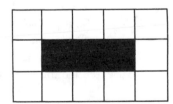

| Length 1 | Length 2 | Length 3 |

Write an expression that describes the number of tiles needed to make a border around a garden of any length. How did you find your expression? Share your expression with a partner. How do your expressions differ? Are they both correct?

Associated guiding questions:

- How does the rule work; how is it helpful?

- How are things changing?

- What steps am I doing over and over?

- Now that I have an equation, how do the numbers (parameters) in the equation relate to the problem context?

- What if I start at the end?

You and your students will come up with a variety of expressions, depending on how you approach the problem. Regardless of approach, all expressions should be equivalent to the following: If x is the length of the garden, then the number of tiles is $2x + 6$.

Finding the simplest form of the expression is not necessarily desirable; in fact, as was the case with Doris and Sums of Consecutive Numbers, it is the expressions that are not in simplified form that often shed the most light on the underlying mathematics. Students will come up with different expressions that reflect different ways of seeing the pattern. Following are expressions students often determine. What might these students be thinking?

- A garden of length x has $2x + 6$ tiles.

- A garden of length x has $2(x + 3)$ tiles.

- A garden of length x has $3(x + 2) - x$ tiles.

Students who are not visual thinkers often create a table and work with numbers alone to come up with an expression. While many will come up with the standard $2x + 6$, others think about it differently. For example, a sixth-grade student with whom we worked came up with this rule: "A garden of length x has $x + 7 + (x - 1)$ tiles." How did he get his rule?

This problem involves gardens of width 1 and any length framed with a single row of tiles, but the problem can be extended by examining gardens that have any width and gardens framed by two or more rows. In addition, the problem can be extended into three dimensions.

Towering Numbers

Like the previous problem, this problem (the first part of which also appears in Chapter 5) invites students to generate many equivalent expressions and to make connections between their expressions and the original context of the problem.

Towering Numbers[7]

```
                  1
               1  2  1
            1  2  3  2  1
         1  2  3  4  3  2  1
      1  2  3  4  5  4  3  2  1
   1  2  3  4  5  6  5  4  3  2  1
1  2  3  4  5  6  7  6  5  4  3  2  1
```

1. There are seven rows in the tower pictured above. How many bricks are in the seventh row?

2. Suppose you wanted to build a tower with 25 rows using the same design. Describe how you could figure out how many bricks you would need for the twenty-fifth (longest) row.

3. A very large tower was built using the same design. The longest row had 299 bricks in it. How many rows of bricks did the tower have?

4. If somebody told you how many rows of bricks were in a tower, how could you figure out the number of bricks in the longest row?

5. If somebody told you how many bricks were in the longest row of a tower, how could you figure out how many rows there were?

6. How many bricks all together are in the tower that is pictured?

7. How many bricks all together would be in the tower in problem 2, which had 25 rows? Tell how you figured out your answer.

8. A large tower has 10,000 bricks all together. How many rows are in the tower? Tell how you figured out your answer.

9. Tell how you could figure out the number of bricks in a tower if someone told you how many rows were in the tower.

10. Tell how you could figure out the number of rows in a tower if someone told you how many bricks were in the tower all together.

Associated guiding questions:

- How does the rule work; how is it helpful?
- When I do the same thing with different numbers, what still holds true? What changes?
- What are my operation shortcuts for getting from here to there?
- What are other ways to write this expression that will bring out hidden meaning?
- Now that I have an equation, how do the numbers (parameters) in the equation relate to the problem context?

The first half of the activity focuses on the relationship between the number of rows in a tower and the length of the longest row. This is yet another activity containing opportunities for the development of many equivalent expressions. Although they might come up with different expressions, students should find that the number of bricks in the nth row is equivalent to $2n - 1$. Some students will "see" the number of bricks as $2(n - 1) + 1$; others will see it as $n + (n - 1)$. What chunking is going on in these students' heads?

The second half of the activity is more challenging. Figure out the number of bricks in a tower with a small number of rows for a few cases. What patterns do you notice in the relationship between the number of rows in the tower and the number of bricks in the tower? After generating only a small number of cases, it becomes clear that the total number of bricks in a tower with n rows is equal to n^2. Unlike the first part of the activity, though, it is not as easy to tell, based on the picture, *why* the total number of bricks is the square of the number of rows.

There are several possible strategies you can use to show that the number of bricks in a tower with n rows is necessarily equal to n^2. First, you could work with numbers alone. You know that the number of bricks in a tower with n rows is equal to the sum of the bricks in each row, and from the first part of the problem, you know how many bricks are in each row. Use this information to write a sum, as in $1 + 3 + 5 + 7 = 16$. (If you worked through the activities in Chapter 3, you will see a connection here to what you did in the Differences of Squares problem.) From that point, you can compute to find that the sum is equal to n^2; as you do this, your thinking reflects Abstracting from Computation. Questions that might help when calculating the sum include the following: How can you write the sum in terms of things you care about? What are your options for operation shortcuts?

Alternatively, you could approach the problem visually to make the connection between the expression and the visual image of the tower. What might a visual representation of the expression n^2 look like? One obvious visual representation of the expression n^2 is an $n \times n$ square. If the total number of bricks is equal to n^2, then there must be a way to rearrange the bricks into an $n \times n$ square.

There are a couple of different ways the tower could systematically be transformed into a square. For example, you could cut off all of the bricks on one side of the middle column of bricks, flip them over, and set them on top of the other side of the tower to get a square. The following diagram illustrates this process for a tower with three rows. (The bricks that are cut off, flipped, and set on top of the other side of the tower are shaded.)

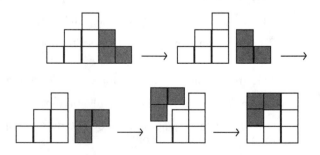

There are also other ways to rearrange the bricks into a square. Find two other ways of manipulating the tower to create a square.

Seeing these arguments helps students to not only develop their own symbol sense, but also begin looking for connections between expressions and other representations in other problems.

In this problem, students were given a visual pattern and then asked to find an expression or equation to describe the pattern. As an extension, you can undo this process by starting with an expression or equation and creating a pattern with squares that the expression or equation could describe. For example, find a pattern with squares such that the nth term of the pattern has $n^2 - 4$ squares.

Notes

1. This activity was developed by Raysa Castillo, Milwaukee Public Schools.
2. Excerpted from *Mathematics in Context: Comparing Quantities*, copyright 1998 by Encyclopaedia Brittanica Educational Corporation.
3. Excerpted from *Mathematics in Context: Comparing Quantities*, copyright 1998 by Encyclopaedia Brittanica Educational Corporation.
4. Excerpted from "Symbol Sense: Informal Sense-Making in Formal Mathematics" by Abraham Arcavi, *For the Learning of Mathematics,* 1994, Vol. 14, No. 3.
5. This activity is adapted from Arcavi, A. 1994. "Symbol Sense: Informal Sense-making in Formal Mathematics." *For the Learning of Mathematics* 14 (3): 25.
6. Excerpted from *MathScape: Seeing and Thinking Mathematically, Patterns in Numbers and Shapes,* copyright 1998 by Creative Publications.
7. Excerpted from *Problem-mathics* by C. Greenes, R. Spungin and J. Dombrowski, copyright 1977 by C. Greenes, published by Creative Publications.

References and Further Reading

Arcavi, A. 1994. "Symbol Sense: Informal Sense-Making in Formal Mathematics." *For the Learning of Mathematics* 14 (3): 24–35.

Demana, F. & J. Leitzel. 1988. "Establishing Fundamental Concepts Through Numerical Problem Solving." In *The Ideas of Algebra, K–12* (1988 Yearbook), ed. A.F. Coxford, 61–68. Reston, VA: NCTM.

English, L.D. & E.A. Warren. 1998. "Introducing the Variable Through Pattern Exploration." *Mathematics Teacher* 91 (2): 166–70.

Fey, J. 1990. "Quantity." In *On the Shoulders of Giants: New Approaches to Numeracy,* ed. L.A. Steen, 61–94. Washington: National Academy Press.

Kieran, C., A. Boileau & M. Garancon. 1996. "Introducing Algebra by Means of a Technology-Supported, Functional Approach." In *Approaches to Algebra: Per-*

spectives for Research and Teaching, eds. N. Bednarz, C. Kieran & L. Lee, 257–94. Dordrecht, The Netherlands: Kluwer Academic Publishers.

Kieran, C. & L. Chalouh. 1993. "Prealgebra: The Transition from Arithmetic to Algebra." In *Research Ideas for the Classroom: Middle Grades Mathematics,* eds. D.T. Owens, 179–98. New York: Macmillan.

Lee, L. 1996. "An Initiation into Algebraic Culture Through Generalization Activities." In *Approaches to Algebra: Perspectives for Research and Teaching,* eds. N. Bednarz, C. Kieran & L. Lee, 87–106. Dordrecht, The Netherlands: Kluwer Academic.

MacGregor, M. & K. Stacey. 1993. "Cognitive Models Underlying Students' Formulation of Simple Linear Equations." *Journal for Research in Mathematics Education* 24 (3): 217–32.

Mason, J. 1996. "Expressing Generality and Roots of Algebra." In *Approaches to Algebra: Perspectives for Research and Teaching,* eds. N. Bednarz, C. Kieran & L. Lee, 65–86. Dordrecht, The Netherlands: Kluwer Academic Publishers.

Patterson, A.C. 1997. "Building Algebraic Expressions: A Physical Model." *Mathematics Teaching in the Middle School* 2 (4): 238–40.

Tall, D. & M. Thomas. 1991. "Encouraging Versatile Thinking in Algebra Using the Computer." *Educational Studies in Mathematics* 22 (2): 125–48.

Taylor, L.J.C. & J.A. Nichols. 1994. "Graphing Calculators Aren't Just for High School Students." *Mathematics Teaching in the Middle School* 1 (3): 190–96.

Wheeler, D. 1996. "Backwards and Forwards: Reflections on Different Approaches to Algebra." In *Approaches to Algebra,* eds. N. Bednarz, C. Kieran & L. Lee, 317–25. Dordrecht, The Netherlands: Kluwer Academic Publishers.

7 *Linking Multiple Representations*

Introduction

One defining feature of algebra is that it "introduces one to a set of tools—tables, graphs, formulas, equations, arrays, identities, functional relations, and so on—that are related to each other sometimes almost interchangeably and together constitute a substantial technology that can be used to discover and invent things" (Wheeler 1996, 322). To master the use of these tools, learners must first understand the associated representations and how to link them together. A fluency in linking and translating among multiple representations seems to be critical in the development of algebraic thinking. The learner who can, for a particular mathematical problem, move fluidly among different mathematical representations has access to a perspective on the mathematics in the problem that is greater than the perspective any one representation can provide. How to help students gain access to such powerful, integrative perspectives—how to help them put the different tools together—is the focus of this chapter.

Teachers in middle grades and early high school will not lack for materials to support students' use of multiple representations. Many of the curricula developed since the advent of the National Council of Teachers of Mathematics (NCTM) Standards reflect the increase in attention to multiple representations, for example, beginning well before formal algebra to require students to use tables and graphs to handle quantitative problems. In addition, technological advancements in the past decade (e.g., graphing calculators, spreadsheets, symbol manipulators) have made it possible to highlight the linking of symbolic, tabular, and graphical representations.

However, even good materials still require teachers to be able to support their students' learning, through the use of timely questions, examples, explanations, and so forth. This chapter looks at some of the considerations for teachers concerning their support of students' use of multiple representations in prealgebra and algebra. With our focus on habits of mind, we pay special attention to the role of multiple representations in helping learners to build rules to represent functions, to abstract from computation, and to have a facility for Doing–Undoing.

141

The role of the teacher in multiple representations is complex, beginning with this consideration: When do I let students develop their own representations, and when do I show them the representations I think are appropriate? As the following story shows, the answer depends, in part, on the teacher's intention.

A Matter of Intention

In a day-long workshop, after an hour of investigating the mathematics in the Sums of Consecutive Numbers activity (see Chapters 2, 3, 4, and 6) a group of high school teachers turned their attention to analyzing several pieces of student work on the same activity. The pieces, selected by the workshop facilitator to illustrate variety in algebraic thinking, were contributed by LUMR project teachers in another city, and so had not been seen by the workshop teachers.

A piece that drew considerable interest appeared, at first glance by the teachers, to demonstrate scattered and not very productive thinking (Figure 7–1). (This example was also shown in Chapter 6.) A teacher in the group, however, argued successfully for a more probing look at the student's effort, which he thought showed signs of algebraic habits of mind in a couple of ways. First, he thought that the student had a way of abstracting something useful from a set of computations and, second, that this abstracting was accomplished by "undoing" whole numbers, like 45, to find sums of consecutive numbers to which they are equal. The teacher

FIGURE 7–1. *Student Work on Sums of Consecutive Number Activity*

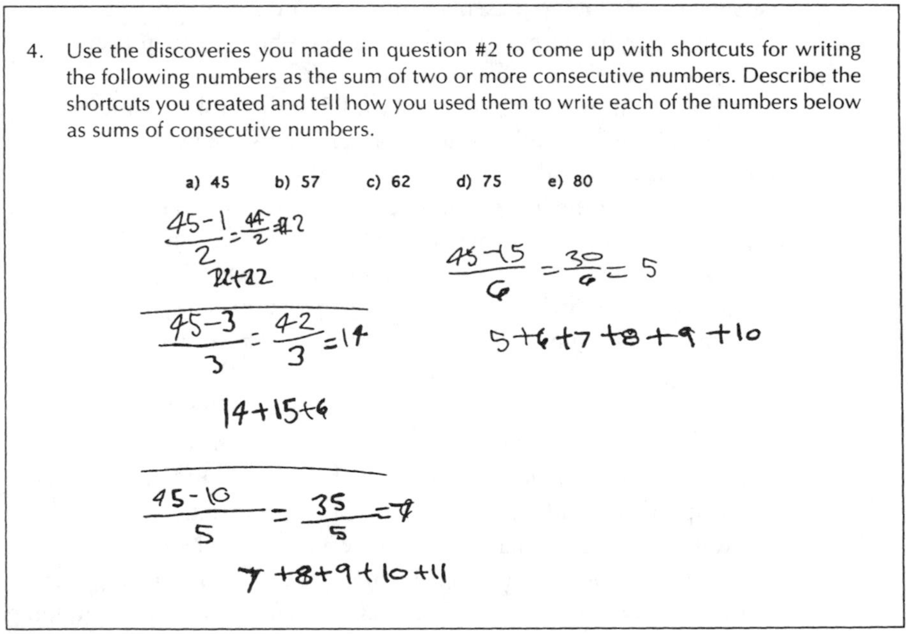

4. Use the discoveries you made in question #2 to come up with shortcuts for writing the following numbers as the sum of two or more consecutive numbers. Describe the shortcuts you created and tell how you used them to write each of the numbers below as sums of consecutive numbers.

a) 45   b) 57   c) 62   d) 75   e) 80

$$\frac{45-1}{2} = \frac{44}{2} = 22$$
$$22+23$$

$$\frac{45-3}{3} = \frac{42}{3} = 14$$
$$14+15+6$$

$$\frac{45-15}{6} = \frac{30}{6} = 5$$
$$5+6+7+8+9+10$$

$$\frac{45-10}{5} = \frac{35}{5} = 7$$
$$7+8+9+10+11$$

argued that it was not too great a leap to infer that the student's undoing of 45 into sums of two, three, five, and six consecutive numbers revealed that the student noticed that three consecutive numbers beginning with any whole number n have the sum $3n + 3$; four consecutive numbers have the sum $4n + 6$; five have the sum $5n + 10$; and so on.

The group was persuaded on this point but, because the student certainly hadn't paid much attention to the directions to "describe the shortcuts" or to "tell how" on any of the pages of his or her work on this problem, there was heated speculation among the teachers as to how the student might have come to this elegant and useful generalization. One of them, Toni, spoke up to say, "Something about that piece of student work bothers me. Unlike the others in the set, that piece provides students a table for organizing the data.[1] I'd never do something like that with my students." "Neither would I," said the teacher next to her, "it ties the kids' hands so you don't see their thinking or how they would approach it." Toni nodded to indicate that that had been her point. The table at issue adjoined the question "What can you discover about the sums of consecutive numbers? Explore and record three discoveries that you can share with the class." It was organized like this, running not to 12, but to 35. (We also have started to fill the table as the student had):

Number	Two Numbers	Three Numbers	Four Numbers	Five Numbers	Six Numbers	Impossible
1						
2						
3	1 + 2					
4						
5	2 + 3					
6		1 + 2 + 3				
7	3 + 4					
8						
9	4 + 5	2 + 3 + 4				
10			1 + 2 + 3 + 4			
11	5 + 6					
12		3 + 4 + 5				

"But," objected a teacher named Jack, "what about the students that need a boost to get them going? I like the fact that the teacher put the table in there. I think the student used the table as a way to get thinking going. Look at the answer to 'What are three discoveries that you can share with the class?' "

1. The higher consecutive numbers are listed, the more space they leave in between.

2. Odd numbers have a better chance to have consecutive numbers than even numbers do.

3. The impossible numbers can be written as 2 to some power.

"The fact that he's talking about 'space' and 'better chance' tells me he's using the table to push his thinking."

This too had its audible support from within the group, but Toni countered, "It's a matter of equity. There are lots of ways to organize mathematical information. I can't expect all students to organize their information the way that I do. Besides, this question is about generalization. I want to see how they think about generalizing." Jack responded to this by saying, "But lots of the kids don't know *how* to generalize and need a starting point. They don't know what to do with open-ended questions like 'What patterns do you see?'" Toni countered with, "But I want to know how they will respond. If I jump to guiding their thinking, I never will. They'll just be organizing things the way I want them to."

At this point, a third teacher, Agnes, spoke up, "But doesn't it make a difference what your purpose is—to assess or to instruct?"

To our ears, as we listened to the discussion, Agnes was right on target: Purpose is at the core of the teacher's role in fostering students' productive use of multiple representations. There will be times that a teacher's purpose is more like Toni's—to see how students organize data to make generalizations—which is more of an assessment purpose. In these cases, it makes sense to abstain from showing representational techniques to the students.

However, as Jack pointed out, the teacher may find that students have no clue how to represent problem data, and so teacher purpose shifts from assessment to instruction. At these moments, when the purpose is instructional, the teacher may choose to show the students how to represent the mathematics with which they are working.

In this particular case, we have no idea how or whether the student used the data in the table to decompose 45 the way he or she did. However, the student could have noticed from the second column that $12 = 3 + (3 + 1) + (3 + 2)$, or $3 \times 3 + 3$, and $15 = 4 + (4 + 1) + (4 + 2)$, or $3 \times 4 + 3$, thus translating from tabular representation to something closer to symbolic representation. Again, we don't know whether the student translated this way. However, it is safe to say that we *want* our students to learn how to translate among representations in this manner.

Reasons for Emphasizing Multiple Representations

It is not so much exposure to different representations that is important for students entering and learning algebra as it is the *linking* of representations and translation among them—for example, figuring a function's equation from the data in its graph, figuring a function's graph from a table of data, and so on. Most elementary school programs expose students to equations and familiarize them with the symbols being used. Similarly, long before they take algebra and before they work with functional relations, students learn the conventions of graphing: In particular, they learn how to plot ordered pairs of numbers as points on a Cartesian graph. However, it appears to be shortsighted, at best, to assume that these casual introductions transfer when students are challenged to handle functional relations or solve equations with unknowns. For example, it may be a mistake to assume that students who are familiar with plotting graphs, point by point, in elementary school will be adequately prepared to see a graph of a function in algebra as representing something whole (the function), as opposed to representing a collection of individual points whose relationship with each other may not be clear to the students (Selden & Selden 1996). Further, most of their exposure to equations in elementary school leads students to believe that equations are statements of *action* ("29 minus 6 makes 23") rather than statements of equivalence or relationship ("y equals $3x + 5$. If $3x + 5$ gets doubled, then so does y"). Therefore, one reason it is important to emphasize for middle and high school students the linking of algebraic representations is to expand or perhaps reorient some of the conceptions they may have developed in elementary school, in particular, to advance their conceptions of equation and function toward being more process-based and less action-focused. In this way, students become more able to treat equations and functions as entities that are manipulable and useful in multiple contexts.

A central theme of this book is the importance of fostering algebraic habits of mind. A facility with translating among representations seems key to acquiring these habits. For example, in Chapter 4 we discussed the value of being able to represent an arithmetic progression such as 11, 26, 41, 56, 71, . . . with the expression $11 + 15n$, where n is understood to cover the nonnegative integers. However, it is equally important to be able to look at an expression such as $11 + 15n$ and recognize that, as n runs through the nonnegative integers, an associated table of numbers is generated, each one 15 greater than its predecessor.

There are other reasons for emphasizing the linking and translating of multiple representations. For example:

- Success in solving algebra problems, especially algebra word problems, depends on both problem representation skills and symbol manipulation skills. "Problem representation skills include constructing and using mathematical representations in words, graphs, tables, and equations. Symbol manipulation skills include being able to carry out arithmetic and algebraic procedures" (Brenner et al. 1997, 666). So, one characteristic of a successful solver of algebra word problems is the ability to translate from verbal, tabular, graphical, and diagrammatic representations into symbolic representations that can be manipulated.

- Translating among tables, equations, and graphs for functions makes it possible for students to understand some key connections among, respectively, arithmetic, algebra, and geometry (Davis 1987). Being able to make these connections would seem to be a critical capacity for students to develop to avoid conceiving of mathematics as a collection of disconnected bits of information and rules.

- In Chapters 2 and 5 we discussed the value of helping students extend beyond their use of arithmetic algorithms to develop habits of building rules to represent functional relations. Key to building such rules is the internalization of the meaning of certain concepts related to functional representation. For example, translating among different representations for functions makes it possible for students to construct a more integrated meaning for key concepts such as "slope" and "y-intercept" (Eisenberg 1992). Hearing the phrase "increasing the slope of a linear function" will trigger for these students a comprehensive sense of what changes this implies for the graph, for the table, and for the equation of the particular linear function.

Each of these reasons points to a recognized hurdle for students learning algebra, so there is ample motivation to make translation among representations an explicit part of students' school mathematics experience. However, it is equally important to do so in ways that maximize the chances of the students understanding.

Issues Regarding Student Understanding

If algebra only comprised discrete pieces of information to be absorbed, it might not be as difficult to understand and use. But, as indicated, there are challenges in thinking algebraically that go beyond learning discrete pieces of information. Some are developmental, in particular, the challenges of *shifting meaning*—for example, the shift of meaning of equation and function from sequences of computational actions to whole processes. Some are conceptual, such as *making connections* between and among different representations. Often, difficulties can arise when it is assumed that students are attaching the same meanings or making the same connections that are intended by teacher or curriculum materials. For example:

1. **Students may not see the links between different representations of a functional relation—for example, the mutual dependence between a function's graph and equation, or between its table and equation.** Even when students are able to write an equation to model a particular functional relation, they may not be able to use it to solve related problems. This is especially true of younger students, who may not see the equation as an object they can manipulate. Working with a group of sixth-graders, Langrall and Swafford (1997) interviewed students as they were presented mathematical situations, such as,

   Mary's basic wage is $20 per week. She is also paid another $2 for each hour of overtime that she works.

   The following interaction was not atypical in the study (15). The student being interviewed had developed a general formula for figuring Mary's total wages, given the number of overtime hours:

Interviewer: "Can you use your formula to find out how much overtime Mary would have to work to earn $50?"

Student: "I don't think so. It is guess and check. . . . You could do it in your head. It would be $30 (overtime) because 20 plus 30 equals 50. So she would have to work 15 overtime hours, because 30 divided by 2 is 15."

There is nothing wrong with such thinking, and one might even speculate that the use of whole numbers in this situation makes it especially convenient for students to figure the answers without having to resort to using equations. Nonetheless, it is still important for teachers to be aware that viewing equations as objects to be operated on and applied—as useful tools—is a capacity that develops gradually in students.

2. **Students may interpret graphs only pointwise, not globally.** This phenomenon often appears in situations in which the graph represents a function of time, and the task is to interpret from the graph how the function varies over time:

    > For example, given a speed versus time graph of a moving car, they can read off the car's speed at a particular time. However, students have much greater difficulty with "across-time questions"; for example, given position versus time graphs of two cars plotted on the same axes, they have great difficulty indicating which one is moving faster at a particular time (Selden & Selden 1992, 13).

    In good part, this phenomenon may be an artifact of students' previous learning experiences. Much of their involvement with graphing in the prealgebra years consists of plotting points one by one on a Cartesian plane, often using tables. This habit could focus and even fix attention on point-to-point interpretations. However, there may also be some deeper difficulties in transferring to the standard Cartesian representation of a function. Goldenberg (1988) points out the possible confusions that can arise when a student moves from a function table, which associates each input number with a unique output number, to a Cartesian graph, which associates each input number with a unique *point* (i.e., a number pair). Students "may recognize fully well that a point may be specified by two coordinates, but may not connect that notion with their *number*-to-*number* representation of function" (Goldenberg 1988, 157). If this confusion is influencing the way learners look at a function's graph, it would impede their capacity to do global interpretations of a graph.

3. **In the course of working on a problem, students may neglect to connect the representations back to the original problem context.** A representation of a word problem, whether by graph, diagram, table, or equation, can become a context unto itself, and students can draw conclusions there that have little to do with the original problem context, and may even contradict the problem's context. Teachers in the Linked Learning project have been made aware of this phenomenon on several occasions. On one occasion, we

gave the teachers a version of the Postage Stamp problem to use for their classroom observations. (Versions of this problem also appear in Chapters 2 and 6.) The underlying mathematics is quite powerful, touching on Diophantine equations and the importance of the concept of relatively prime integers. In its highest level, it is meant to have students wonder about and investigate the following: For what whole-number values of p and q will $mp + nq$, for m,n any integers, result in all but a finite number of integer values?

The teachers' classes spanned grades 6 through 10, so we scaffolded the task to help younger students enter into it, by presenting a grid on which to compute combinations. Here is how the problem began:

Postage Stamp Problem

The post office has only 3-cent and 4-cent stamps. They would like to make a table showing the postage amounts for different combinations of stamps. They have started the table below. Finish filling in the table. Explain what the number inside the shaded box tells a customer.

Postage Amounts for Different Combinations of 3¢ and 4¢ Stamps

Number of 3¢ stamps

	0	1	2	3	4	5	6	7
0	0	3	6					
1	4	7	10					
2	8	11	14					
3								
4		☐						
5				☐				
6						▨		
7								☐

(Number of 4¢ stamps — vertical axis label)

The intention was to help the students organize enough data so that they could engage productively with subsequent questions about the stamp combinations, such as, "Can you make 50 cents postage? 51 cents postage? What postage amounts can you make with 3-cent and 4-cent stamps?" Later in the problem, other stamp values are considered. For many students, however, the task became one of filling in the table according to cues they found there (e.g., "The numbers going across are increasing by 3 each time"), rather than a task of considering number combinations. This dilemma was reported by teachers on the project's electronic network:

Teacher A: What seemed to happen with students (during my observations) was that they filled the table by noting how the columns and rows (that came with some entries filled) were "growing" and continued the patterns without connecting these patterns to the value of the stamps. That is why they probably had such difficulty reversing the process. Even when certain students were "told" that the table displayed the "value" of the stamps, some then saw nothing wrong with saying that the 39 cents came from 13 3-cent stamps. Did anyone begin the prompt with a completely empty table?

Teacher B (in response): I did the postage stamp problem with my students today. Many of the students had the interpretation problem that (Teacher A) talked about. They could fill in the table correctly, but when it came to interpreting what the number in the square meant, they were stuck. Many said that was the number of stamps until I challenged them. Like (Teacher A) said, I needed to go to one of the boxes in the upper left-hand column and ask them what the 3 meant, what the 4 meant, and what the 7 meant.

It would have been shortsighted to treat this dilemma as only a case of an activity that needed reconstructing. The students were telling us something more general: If they do not see the connection between a representation of a problem and the original verbal representation of the problem, then they may work only within the world of the representation and make conclusions that have little to do with the original context.

Ideally, we want students to make their own representations of problems. However, the core message of this chapter is that it is not enough to teach individual representation to students. Good judgment needs to be developed, as well: "Because each representational format has varying limitations or strengths in different contexts, it is beneficial to have the choice of which representations to employ and the knowledge needed to make such a choice" (Lloyd & Wilson 1998, 253). The next section looks at some teaching suggestions for helping students develop good judgment about representations, in particular, as a tool for algebraic thinking.

Bringing Balance to the Use of Representations

Chapter 1 discussed, in general, the role of teacher questions in fostering students' algebraic thinking. Teacher questioning has a particular role to play in helping students make connections in and balance their use of representations of functions—verbal, tabular, graphical, and symbolic. A view inside one classroom might help to create a vision of how this can happen. Researchers in a study of one teacher's efforts to implement a 6-week functions unit from a new curriculum observed of the teacher:

He demonstrated connections by attending to the varied appearances of a particular feature of a relationship in the different representations. For example, numerous students asked Mr. Allen for help with describing the meanings of the numbers in a velocity equation, $V = 25 - 9.8T$. In response, Mr. Allen often related the students' equation, table, and graph to elucidate the role of the equation's numbers in the situation, as reflected in the following discussion:

Lisa: What does the minus nine point eight stand for?

Mr. Allen: Well, what was happening to the graph?

Melanie: It was decreasing.

Mr. Allen: Was it decreasing at the same rate each time?

Melanie: I don't know.

Mr. Allen: Well, let's check and see. Let's calculate the difference between the table values. What are the increments?

Lisa: The increment is nine point eight.

Mr. Allen: Nine point eight what?

Lisa: Well, the velocity is going down by nine point eight meters per second each time. (Lloyd & Wilson 1998, 266)

The student's question had to do with meaning in the equation. Rather than just answer the question directly, the teacher brought the students' attention to the graph, then to the table, giving them a chance to weave the graphical information with the tabular information for an answer to the student's question about the data in the equation.

Helping students draw information about a function's equation from its graph is especially important. For example, constructing the graph of a linear function, point to point, is generally far easier than going in the other direction. Like Mr. Allen, teachers need to help students look for relevant information in a line's graph, in particular, to conceptualize "point plus slope as line rather than point to point as line" (Leinhardt, Zaslavsky & Stein 1990, 46), and to help them also connect this conceptualization to the linear function's equation and table.

Also important is helping students to distinguish features of a function's graph that are indigenous to the graph itself (e.g., the y-intercept) from features that are not indigenous (e.g., the slope of a linear function's graph can change depending on the scale, as can the shape of a parabolic function).

To help students take a global approach to thinking about function graphs, in addition to their thinking about them in pointwise fashion, teachers can engage students in discussions that focus attention on how quantities vary, and how the variations are represented in the graphs. Nemirovsky (1996) cites an example used in his research work (295):

Suppose that two cars move according to the following graph of velocity versus time:

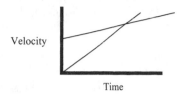

Velocity   Time

How do you imagine movement of the two cars? Do the initial positions matter? How? Do they meet? When? Is one of the cars ahead of the other?

Experiences like these can focus students' attention on variational and global information. A good source of such activities is *The Language of Functions and Graphs* (Shell Centre for Mathematics Education 1985).

As indicated previously, a part of student sense-making in their use of multiple representations is to hold onto an awareness of the original problem contexts. Our example of the postage stamps activity indicates that one factor in helping students is to make sure that mathematical problems are not constructed to make it easy for students to reason about data totally divorced from original conditions. In the Linked Learning project, we also related this aspect of student sense-making to standards for *convincing argument* on the part of students. In particular, we suggested to teachers that they attend to whether students are relating their reasoning back to the question being answered, *even if* the answer obtained is basically correct. For example, the following three student responses are on target, but the first one answers according to a numerical table set up—"× [times] by 2 subtract 1"—while the other two relate their answers to how the tower is being built with the bricks. The activity they worked on was the Towering Numbers problem (see Chapters 5 and 6):

Student 1 Response

Suppose you wanted to build a tower with 25 rows using the same design. Describe how you could figure out how many bricks you would need for the twenty-fifth (longest) row.

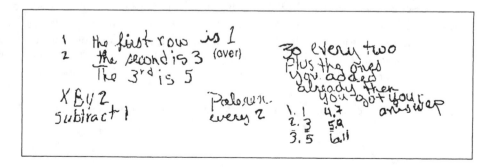

Student 2 Response

Suppose you wanted to build a tower with 25 rows using the same design. Describe how you could figure out how many bricks you would need for the twenty-fifth (longest) row.

I would make my tower. I know that the twenty-fifth block is the middle block, and that there is one less block on each side, which would make it 24 blocks on each side. If you multiply 24 by 2 and add the middle block, you get 49 blocks.

Student 3 Response

A very large tower was built using the same design. The longest row had 299 bricks in it. How many rows of bricks did the tower have? Tell how you figured out your answer.

150 rows. We knew that both sides added together equaled 299, that the middle number made it equal an odd number. So you take one off and have 298. Then since you have two sides you divided 298 by 2, which equals 149 on each side, and then you have to add one block for the one you took away, and have 150.

Again, in this particular case, our point is not that the first student got into mathematical trouble by leaving the context behind. Rather, our point is that there are instances in which such trouble can arise; therefore, teachers need to (1) attend to what students are paying attention to as they work with different representations, and (2) make students aware that there are standards for convincing arguments in mathematics, in particular, connecting back to problem statement and context.

Lastly, we recognize that the growing role of technology in fostering algebraic thinking is promising support to students' making connections and bringing balance to their use of multiple representations. Reporting on a series of studies involving computer-supported introductions to algebra, Kieran, Boileau, and Garancon (1996) suggest that the use of technology not only makes guess-and-check strategies more attractive to middle-grades students than they are when students are working by hand, but also, as a result, "provide students with the opportunity to link algebra problem solving with their earlier arithmetic knowledge and experience" (261). Additionally, many researchers (e.g., Goldenberg 1988; Kieran, Boileau, and Garancon 1996) have pointed to the power of automated graphing tools to help learners focus on the graph as a whole and to actively link representations of functions, thus, perhaps, facilitating their development of a conception of functions as processes, not actions. As we have noted elsewhere, this shift in conception of function is one of the most critical shifts in algebraic thinking that learners can make in learning introductory algebra (see, e.g., Cuoco 1992).

Example Activities

Following are activities we feel can help students develop the ability to create and interpret different mathematical representations.

Juan and Marina Go Walking

Activities that give students opportunities to translate between different representations can help them better understand the meaning of each individual representation. In this activity, students must coordinate information from four different graphs to come up with a story that is consistent with each graph.

Juan and Marina Go Walking[2]
Write an imaginative story that matches the information on the graphs below. Use information from all four of the graphs.

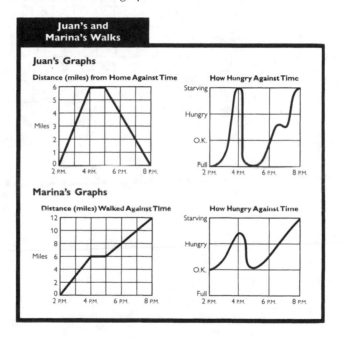

Many different answers are possible. In all, however, the question, "How are things changing?" guides thinking. Noticing differences is also important, in particular, the distinction between Juan's and Marina's graphs representing distance walked: Juan's graph measures his distance *from* home, while Marina's represents total miles walked. Is it possible that Juan and Marina were together during the time represented? Why or why not?

Matching

This problem requires making judgments about the connection between tables of data and graphs without plotting points. It encourages a more global view of the two representations. It also can help solidify an understanding of the implicit relationships between the two representations.

Matching[3]

Without plotting, choose the best sketch graph to fit each of the tables shown below. Particular graphs may fit more than one table. Copy the most suitable graph, name the axes clearly, and explain your choice. If you cannot find the graph you want, draw your own version.

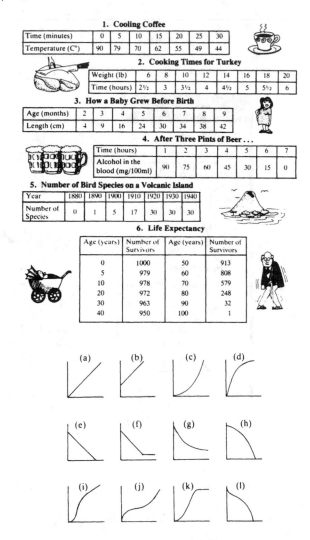

1. Cooling Coffee

Time (minutes)	0	5	10	15	20	25	30
Temperature (C°)	90	79	70	62	55	49	44

2. Cooking Times for Turkey

Weight (lb)	6	8	10	12	14	16	18	20
Time (hours)	2½	3	3½	4	4½	5	5½	6

3. How a Baby Grew Before Birth

Age (months)	2	3	4	5	6	7	8	9
Length (cm)	4	9	16	24	30	34	38	42

4. After Three Pints of Beer . . .

Time (hours)	1	2	3	4	5	6	7
Alcohol in the blood (mg/100ml)	90	75	60	45	30	15	0

5. Number of Bird Species on a Volcanic Island

Year	1880	1890	1900	1910	1920	1930	1940
Number of Species	0	1	5	17	30	30	30

6. Life Expectancy

Age (years)	Number of Survivors	Age (years)	Number of Survivors
0	1000	50	913
5	979	60	808
10	978	70	579
20	972	80	248
30	963	90	32
40	950	100	1

By asking for answers that match tables and graphs without plotting points, the problem asks the solver to pay attention to features of tabular data that give clues about the underlying relationship between the variables represented in the table. (Is there information here that can help me predict? How can I predict what's going to happen without doing all the calculation?) For each table, you must compare the relative rate of increase or decrease of the two variables and translate this into a graphical representation, or vice versa. Were you conscious of when you were using clues from the graphs to investigate the tables, and when you were using clues from the tables to investigate the graphs? When you use the problem in class, ask students similar kinds of questions about their thinking: what information they used; what prediction clues they paid attention to; when their thinking went from table to graph; and when their thinking went from graph to table.

The following graphs match the tables:

1. Cooling Coffee: g

2. Cooking Times for Turkey: b (assuming the horizontal axis starts at 6 lb.)

3. How a Baby Grew Before Birth: i

4. After Three Pints of Beer . . . : e

5. Number of Bird Species on a Volcanic Island: k

6. Life Expectancy: l

Translations

Like the last activity, the Translations problem encourages a broader perspective on the relationship between tables and graphs than is the traditional fare provided students and teachers. Rather than the familiar task of creating graphs from tables, this problem requires the reverse process based on a global view of the situation.

Translations[4]
Make up tables of numbers that will correspond to the following six graphs:

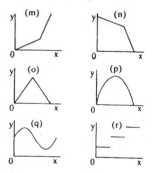

Various tables of numbers are possible, guided in their construction by questions such as, "How are things changing?" and "What is the reverse process?" (i.e., reversing the process of plotting points from data on a table). Compare the tables of data for each graph. What do the tables of data have in common? (For example, each graph has at least one critical point where direction changes or there is a discontinuity.) How are they different? (For example, some are made from straight line segments; others aren't.) When students do this activity, ask similar questions. Such a comparison not only helps students learn more about each representation, but also provides students with opportunities to seek and express patterns and, in their comparison, to abstract important features of the graphical and tabular patterns.

An Integral Part

Here is a challenge that can be approached through different representations. Some will want to work with the equation representation, while others will manipulate the graphical representation to come up with an answer.

An Integral Part[5]

The straight line $y = (7/15)x + 1/3$ passes through two points with integral coordinates (10,5) and (−20, −9). Are there other "integral points" (points with integral coordinates) on this straight line?

Solving the problem graphically requires manipulating key geometric features of the graph, to arrive at an answer and to see some of the structure that underlies the building of this linear functional rule. Draw the line on graph paper and then mark points to represent (10,5) and (−20, −9). (What information is here that can help me predict what will happen?) The right triangle that goes along with this line and these points has a horizontal side of 30 units and a vertical side of 14 units. Students can then use similar triangles to find another point with integral coordinates. (What steps am I doing over and over again?)

It is also possible to approach the problem without ever graphing it, by looking only at the equation. In this case, it becomes possible to do some Abstracting from Computation (How can I predict what is going to happen without doing all the calculation? What are other ways to write that expression that will bring out hidden meaning?) and to move toward addressing a more general challenge: Characterize all integral points on this line. One way to think about it is to change the expression and think in terms of modular arithmetic: Saying that $(7/15)x + 1/3$ is an integer, for x also is an integer, is the same as saying $7x/15 + 1/3$ is an integer, which means that $7x$ will leave a remainder of 10 when divided by 15. So, $(x, (7/15)x + 1/3)$ is an "integral point" if and only if x is of the form $10 + 15m$ for some integer m.

Graphing GCD Relationships

It is possible to become more fluent in representing functional relations by examining representations of nonstandard functional relations, as in the following problem's functions, the domain and range of which are discrete points. By comparing how these functions can be represented by graphs, tables, and equations, one can gain a better understanding of each representation.

Graphing GCD Relationships[6]

1. a. Complete the table given below for the relationship $f(x) = GCD(3,x)$

x	1	2	3	4	5	6
$f(x)$						

b. Graph the relationship $f(x) = GCD(3,x)$ where x is a positive integer.

c. Is f a function? Why or why not?

d. Make at least three observations about the graph of f.

2. a. Graph $g(x) = GCD(12,x)$, where x is a positive integer.

b. How are the graphs of f and g alike? How are they different?

c. What can you say about the values of g?

d. Use the graph of g to predict the value of $g(40)$. Explain your answer.

3. The graph below represents the function $m(x) = GCD(k,x)$ for some constant k < 10. Determine this value of k.

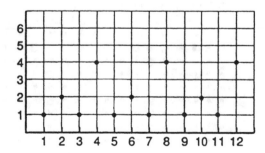

When you use this activity with students, be sure that students understand why they should not connect the dots on the graph. Following are the graphs for 1b and 2a:

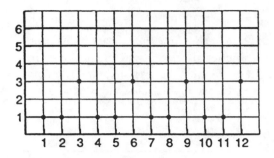 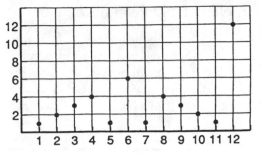

To make observations about the graphs is to be guided by questions such as these: What steps am I doing over and over? When I do the same thing with different numbers, what changes; what stays the same? How can I describe the graph without using specific inputs? Similar questions can be used with students. As students answer your questions and make their thinking visible, be sure that they talk about how these functions are periodic and have domains and ranges that are discrete points. In the last part of the problem, item 3, the challenge is to switch from doing to undoing. What process reverses the one I have been using? The k value for item 3 is 4.

Pattern Seeking with Spreadsheets

Spreadsheet software provides yet another context in which to examine the concept of functions and patterns. A spreadsheet constitutes a representation in its own right, and it can help solidify the input–output conception of function.

Pattern Seeking with Spreadsheets[7]
Consider the following sequence:

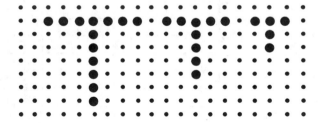

1. Using a spreadsheet application, find the next three terms in the sequence, the 15th term, the 50th term, and the nth term.

2. Find the position in the sequence of the largest construct that you can make from 1000 dots. What is the exact number of items that you must use for this purpose?

Guiding question: How can I describe the steps without using specific inputs? The nth term in this pattern has $4n + 1$ dots. This kind of problem can be done with a wide range of patterns. Spreadsheet software is especially useful for comparing equivalent expressions—for example, $4n + 1$ and $2n + (2n + 1)$. (What are other ways to write that expression to bring out hidden meaning?) Spreadsheet software also allows students to quickly generate tables of data representing different types of functions, thus allowing them to develop their function sense.

Snakes in Snakewood

It is important to be familiar with the four standard ways of representing situations in algebra: expressions and equations, graphs, tables, and words. However, it is equally important to be able to create other problem-specific representations when necessary. The following problem invites the use of a different kind of representation, one that is not one of the standard four but that can be used in many problems dealing with recursive relationships.

Snakes in Snakewood[8]

Snakes in Snakewood have colored rings around the tail that follow a changing pattern. As snakes grow older, the pattern extends in a systematic way.

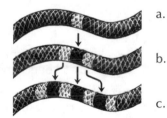

a.

b.

c.

a. It starts with a white ring.

b. Then a black ring develops in the middle of the white ring.

c. In the next stage, the same thing happens with each white ring, but the black rings stay the same.

The process continues in the same way as the snake grows older.

1. You've seen the first three stages in the ring pattern. What are the fourth and fifth stages?

2. What is the relationship between the numbers of white and black rings in each string?

3. A snake has 128 white rings. How many rings does the snake have in total?

4. Another snake has 255 black rings. How many total rings does this snake have?

5. Is it possible for this kind of snake to have 499 rings? Why or why not?

This problem invites a different kind of representation from the standard four: graphs, equations, tables, and words. If W represents a white ring and B represents a black ring, then the rule can be represented by: $W \rightarrow WBW$; $B \rightarrow B$, and the first three stages can be represented as follows:

$W \rightarrow WBW \rightarrow WBW\,B\,WBW$. (How does the rule work? What steps am I doing over and over? How can I describe the steps without using specific inputs?)

At each stage, there is always one less black ring than there are white rings. In fact, the number of white rings in the nth stage is equal to 2^{n-1}, and the number of black rings in the nth stage is equal to $2^{n-1} - 1$. The rule indicates that for every white ring in a given stage, there are twice as many white rings in the next stage. Because there is 1 white ring at the first stage and the white rings double at every stage, there must be 2^{n-1} white rings at the nth stage.

Candle Problem

Like Snakes in Snakewood, this problem invites using nonstandard representations, in this case, a pictorial representation.

Candle Problem[9]

1. Maria has a red candle and a green candle. Each candle is 18 cm long. Maria lit each candle at the same time. The red candle took 6 hours to burn out, but the green candle took 3 hours to burn out.

   a. After one hour of burning, which candle was longer? How much longer? Explain how you got your answer.

   b. After how much time was one of the candles exactly twice as long as the other? Explain how you got your answer.

2. Two candles of equal length are lit at the same time. One candle takes 6 hours to burn out, and the other takes 9 hours to burn out. After how much time will the slower burning candle be exactly twice as long as the faster burning one? Explain how you got your answer.

The several parts of this problem can be approached by setting up rate equations. However, they epitomize the point made in an earlier section: that success in solving algebra word problems depends on *both* problem representation skills and symbol manipulation skills.

It is also possible to represent the situation visually and manipulate their representation to arrive at an answer. For example, the following diagram is useful in solving the second question:

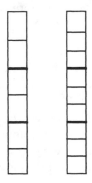

The candle on the left represents the candle that burns in 6 hours, and the candle on the right represents the candle that burns in 9 hours. Each marking represents an hour of burning. After 1 hour, one segment from each candle has burned. With this representation, how can you tell when the slower burning candle is twice as long as the faster burning candle? If you compare them after 4 hours, that point in time hasn't yet been reached. On the other hand, after 5 hours, that point has been passed. Is the critical point exactly 4.5 hours? The answer is yes, and you can convince yourself by noting that 1 of the hour chunks in the left-hand candle is equal to 1.5-hour chunks of the right-hand candle. Your students may very well use this picture-based reasoning process to solve the problem. Is it algebraic thinking? Yes, at least implicitly, because it is reasoning based on the recognition that the starting length of the candles doesn't matter, thinking that responds to the questions, "When I do the same thing with different numbers, what still holds true? What changes?" It also responds to the question, "How are things changing?" and, if the students make the observation that 1 chunk on the left is equivalent to 1.5 chunks on the right, they are responding to the fundamental question, "Is there a relationship here?"

A more symbolic approach to the second part of the problem might be to let L equal the length of each candle, and to recognize that the length of the slower burning candle after t hours is $L - (tL/9)$ and the length of the other candle after t hours is $L - (tL/6)$. Then it is a matter of setting the appropriate equation: $L - (tL/9) = 2[L - (tL/6)]$. The L cancels out (revealing that the starting length doesn't matter), and solving for t, we find the answer 4.5.

Around the Horn

This problem requires a focused effort to represent the information in the problem. It gives practice coming up with new representations and then working within them to arrive at a solution.

Around the Horn[10]

Many families from the eastern United States migrated to California in the 1800s. Instead of going overland to reach California, some families migrated west by taking a ship that went around Cape Horn at the tip of South America. Suppose a ship leaves New York for San Francisco on the first of every month at noon, and, at the same time, a ship leaves San Francisco for New York. Suppose also that each ship arrives exactly 6 months after it leaves. If you were on a ship leaving from New York, how many ships from San Francisco would you meet?

The first consideration in solving this problem is to determine what counts as a *meeting*. As each ship leaves port, another returns. Does this initial contact, leaving port, count as a meeting? What is decided is not important; rather, it is important to make the interpretation and any other assumptions clear, and then provide reasoning to support the answer.

Drawing some kind of visual representation of the situation is important. For example, the following diagram may be useful:

1	2	3	4	5	6	7	Month 1
g	f	e	d	c	b	a	

2	3	4	5	6	7	8	Month 2
h	g	f	e	d	c	b	

Each letter and number represent a boat, and suppose San Francisco is on one side of the line, while New York is on the other. Then the above diagram represents the placement of ships at noon on the first of months 1 and 2. From the diagram, it is clear that from month 1 to month 2, each moving boat passes two boats moving in the opposite direction.

When you do this activity with students, they may do such a diagram, or they may want to act out the scenario with other people or use manipulatives to come up with an answer. Regardless of the representation with which students work, they should get that a boat will pass 13 other ships on its journey to the other side of the country, assuming that we count any boat seen, including those seen when leaving or arriving.

Here are some extensions, which elicit more algebraic thinking by changing some of the variables: How many ships would you pass in n months? What if ships going in one direction went twice as fast as ships going in the other direction? How many ships would you pass?

Notes

1. In the LUMR project, we typically gave participating teachers the latitude they requested in adapting the mathematics activities to their needs, and asked only that they not scaffold them so much that individual student thinking fails to shine through.
2. Excerpted from *MathScape: Seeing and Thinking Mathematically, Mathematics of Motion,* copyright 1998 by Creative Publications.
3. This material is copied from *Language of Functions and Graphs,* page 110, originally published by the Shell Centre, Nottingham and now available from QED of York (England) at +44-1904-424242 and qed@enterprise.net
4. This material is copied from *Language of Functions and Graphs,* page 110, originally published by the Shell Centre, Nottingham and now available from QED of York (England) at +44-1904-424242 and qed@enterprise.net
5. This activity is from Gelfand, I.M., E.G. Glagoleva & E.E. Shnol. 1990. *Functions and Graphs,* 24. Boston: Birkhauser.
6. Excerpted from "Functions and Their Representations" by K. G. Graham and J. Ferrini-Murdy, *Mathematics Teacher,* 1990, Vol. 83, No. 3.
7. Excerpted from "An EXCELlent Bridge to Algebra" by Alex Friedlander, *Mathematics Teacher,* 1998, Vol. 91, No. 5.
8. Excerpted from *Mathematics in Context: Patterns and Symbols,* copyright 1998 by Encyclopaedia Britannica Educational Corporation.
9. This activity is adapted from Kroll, D.L., J.O. Masingila & S.T. Mau. 1992. "Cooperative Problem Solving: But What About Grading?" *Arithmetic Teacher* 39 (6): 20.
10. Excerpted from "The Overland Trail," *Interactive Mathematics Program Year 1,* copyright 1997 by Interactive Mathematics Program. Published by Key Cirriculum Press (Emeryville, CA).

References and Further Reading

Brenner, M. et al. 1997. "Learning by Understanding: The Role of Multiple Representations in Learning Algebra." *American Educational Research Journal* 34 (4): 663–89.

Cuoco, A. 1992. *Action to Process: Constructing Functions from Algebra Word Problems.* Newton, MA: Education Development Center.

Davis, R. 1987. "Theory and Practice." *Journal of Mathematical Behavior* 6 (1): 97–126.

Edwards, T.G. 1996. "Exploring Quadratic Functions: From a to c." *Mathematics Teacher* 89 (2): 144–46.

Eisenberg, T. 1992. "On the Development of a Sense for Functions." In *The Concept of Function: Aspects of Epistemology and Pedagogy.* MAA Notes, Volume 25, eds. G. Harel & E. Dubinsky, 153–74. Washington, D.C.: Mathematical Association of America.

Goldenberg, E.P. 1988. "Mathematics, Metaphors, and Human Factors: Mathematical, Technical, and Pedagogical Challenges in the Educational Use of Graphical Representation of Functions." *Journal of Mathematical Behavior* 7 (2): 135–73.

Goolsby, R.C. & T.W. Polaski. 1997. "Extraneous Solutions and Graphing Calculators." *Mathematics Teacher* 90 (9): 718–20.

Harel, G. & E. Dubinsky, eds. 1992. *The Concept of Function: Aspects of Epistemology and Pedagogy.* MAA Notes, Volume 25. Washington, D.C.: Mathematical Association of America.

Heid, M.K. 1990. "Uses of Technology in Prealgebra and Beginning Algebra." *Mathematics Teacher* 83 (3): 194–98.

Kieran, C., A. Boileau & M. Garancon. 1996. "Introducing Algebra by Means of a Technology-Supported, Functional Approach." In *Approaches to Algebra: Perspectives for Learning and Teaching,* eds. N. Bednarz, C. Kieran & L. Lee, 257–94. Dordrecht, The Netherlands: Kluwer Academic Publishers.

Langrall, C.W. & J.O. Swafford. 1997. "Grade Six Students' Use of Equations to Describe and Represent Problem Situations." Paper presented at the annual meeting of the American Educational Research Association, Chicago, Illinois, March 1997.

Leinhardt, G., O. Zaslavsky & M.K. Stein. 1990. "Functions, Graphs, and Graphing: Tasks, Learning, and Teaching." *Review of Educational Research* 60 (1): 1–64.

Lloyd, G.M. & M. Wilson. 1998. "Supporting Innovation: The Impact of a Teacher's Conceptions of Functions on His Implementation of a Reform Curriculum." *Journal for Research in Mathematics Education* 29 (3): 248–74.

Nemirovsky, R. 1996. "A Functional Approach to Algebra: Two Issues That Emerge." In *Approaches to Algebra: Perspectives for Learning and Teaching,* eds. N. Bednarz, C. Kieran & L. Lee, 295–316. Dordrecht, The Netherlands: Kluwer Academic Publishers.

Selden, A. & J. Selden. 1992. "Research Perspectives on Conceptions of Function: Summary and Overview." In *The Concept of Function: Aspects of Epistemology and Pedagogy.* MAA Notes, Volume 25, eds. G. Harel & E. Dubinsky, 1–21. Washington, D.C.: Mathematical Association of America.

Shell Centre for Mathematical Education. 1985. *The Language of Functions and Graphs.* Nottingham, England: Shell Centre for Mathematical Education. (Now available from QED of York (England) at +44-1904-424242 and qed@enterprise.net)

Simon, M.A. & V.C. Stimpson. 1988. "Developing Algebraic Representations Using Diagrams." In *The Ideas of Algebra, K–12: 1988 Yearbook,* ed. A. Coxford, 136–41. Reston, VA: NCTM.

Wheeler, D. 1996. "Backwards and Forwards: Reflections on Different Approaches to Algebra." In *Approaches to Algebra: Perspectives for Learning and Teaching,* eds. N. Bednarz, C. Kieran & L. Lee, 317–25. Dordrecht, The Netherlands: Kluwer Academic Publishers.

Yerushalmy, M. & S. Gilead. 1997. "Solving Equations in a Technological Environment." *Mathematics Teacher* 90 (2): 156–62.

INDEX